BLUEPRINT
for
INVESTMENT

2nd Edition

BLUEPRINT
for
INVESTMENT

2nd Edition

RICHARD FITZHERBERT

Wrightbooks

Wrightbooks Pty Ltd
PO Box 270
Elsternwick
Victoria 3185
Ph: (03) 9532 7082   Fax: (03) 9532 7084   Email: wbooks@ozemail.com.au

National Library of Australia Cataloguing-in-publication data:

FitzHerbert, Richard
BluePrint for Investment 2nd Ed.
Includes index.
ISBN 1 875857 54 0
1. Investments - Australia. 2. Investment analysis.
I. Title.
332.63

Cover design by Rob Cowpe
Printed in Australia by Australian Print Group
ISBN: 1 875857 54 0

NOTE

The material in this book is of the nature of general comment only, and neither purports nor intends to be advice. Readers should not act on the basis of any matter in this book without considering (and, if appropriate, taking) professional advice with due regard to their own particular circumstances. The decision to trade and the method of trading is for the reader alone. The author and publisher expressly disclaim all and any liability to any person, whether a purchaser of this publication or not, in respect of anything and of the consequences of anything done or omitted to be done by any such person in reliance, whether whole or partial, upon the whole or any part of the contents of this publication.

Contents

Chapter 1

INTRODUCTION – DIFFERENT APPROACHES TO INVESTMENT THEORY AND PRACTICE

Chapter 2

THE LESSONS OF HISTORY

Chapter 3

GENERAL FEATURES OF DIFFERENT ASSET CLASSES 57

Chapter 4

INVESTMENT OBJECTIVES AND STRATEGY; FORMULATION, IMPLEMENTATION AND SUPERVISION 83

CONTENTS (Cont'd)

Preface

WHAT *BLUEPRINT FOR INVESTMENT* SEEKS TO ACHIEVE

THIS BOOK is written for the benefit of serious investors and people who, as trustees of estates or superannuation funds, become responsible for money belonging to other people.

For experienced professionals, investment is not an easy task. The newcomer has to cope with an investment world charged with seductive advertising, glossy brochures and persuasive prose. Theories and fallacies are readily assumed as facts. Irrational analysis is reinforced by fads and fashions. Major blunders are committed by senior people and prestigious institutions. As a protection against incompetence and malpractice, government regulation and licensing is acknowledged as providing no guarantees.

BluePrint for Investment attempts to provide the necessary background and historical depth to facilitate unemotional judgement of the various ideas, advice, opinions and 'recommendations' with which investors are bombarded. Sometimes these opinions come from unlikely sources and are not necessarily intended as investment comment. For example, in a letter to the editor of *The Australian Financial Review* of 7 October 1997, Cheryl Kernot, the popular senator and leader of the Australian Democrats at the time, complained about the long-term budgetary effects of the partial privatisation of Telstra Corporation. She wrote:

> "The lucky million or so Australians who can afford to fork out $2,000 for a parcel of Telstra shares at an outrageously undervalued price offered by the Government will be subsidised by the 17 million other Australians left with the $600 million higher tax bill."

The purpose of this quotation is not to discuss the political argument, but to suggest that a senator's opinion that Telstra shares were *"outrageously undervalued"* may have been of interest to potential applicants in the public offer. This book aims to introduce the conscientious non-professional investor or policy-maker to fundamental principles from a context in which he or she can exercise rational judgement when required.

Market conditions at the time of writing in 1997 provided some unusual opportunities to illustrate some of the points under discussion, particularly the risks of speculative bubbles. In this respect, the purpose of *BluePrint for Investment* is to assist readers in forming their own opinion on these matters in the unknown circumstances of the future, rather than to provide immediate answers which will quickly become out of date as circumstances change.

GENERAL APPROACH

The text begins with an examination of some of the theories, ideas and fallacies which make the investment world so interesting for the bystander, and so potentially dangerous (and profitable) for the investor. The historical record is then examined for clues as to when markets go haywire and how the worst excesses can be avoided.

The world is not (yet!) run by computers and robots. In particular, corporate management and portfolio investment decisions are made by normal people who exhibit all sorts of human failings and habits including susceptibility to peer-group pressure, greed, fear and self-interest. The investor needs to understand how human behaviour, group dynamics and mob psychology affect decisions relevant to capital market activity.

With this background *BluePrint* examines the features of different sorts of investments and suggests how prudent people should go about investing their own money or — in the case of trustees — funds entrusted to their care.

For the benefit of trustees of private or excluded superannuation funds, the investment requirements of current Australian superannuation legislation are given some emphasis where relevant to the topic under discussion.

THE OSTRICHES OF 1997

The discussion of speculative bubbles is much more interesting if a recent or current bubble can be found to illustrate the symptoms. At the time of writing the first edition in 1992, major capital markets seemed reasonably sensible and it was necessary to look beyond traditional investments to illustrate the points under discussion. The exotic example of ostriches was dictated by the circumstances of the time and, to the extent that we can rely on advertisements published in rural newspapers, the price of breeding stock seems to have fallen at least 90% since publication of the first edition.

In 1997, the task of finding a speculative bubble to illustrate the discussion was much easier — the US stock market. If readers combine the historic fundamentals and the more interesting psychological evidence, they may conclude that the price level in mid 1997 may have been comparable to levels reached in 1929.

In the final analysis, history will judge this assessment and the arguments are presented for readers to consider and either accept or reject as they see fit.

INVESTMENT THEORIES AND QUANTITATIVE TECHNIQUES

The popularity of undergraduate courses in investment theory, widespread ownership of personal computers, ready availability of spreadsheet software and access to data in electronic form have led to increased interest in investment theory and computer applications.

A very significant proportion of private wealth is invested indirectly through managed funds, superannuation and other forms of collective investment. Many of the decision-makers have been trained in theoretical aspects of investment and mathematical methods.

Discussion of these theories and their assumptions is woven into the text where it is relevant. In addition, this edition contains a new chapter suggesting an alternative theoretical framework for quantitative analysis (Chapter 8).

While many investors may prefer to leave investment theory and the associated calculations to those with an interest in the subject, the use of numerical techniques is becoming more widespread. Understanding the assumptions on which these calculations are based will therefore assist serious private investors. In the case of superannuation fund trustees who act on quantitative advice, it could be argued that gaining this understanding of the underlying assumptions is an obligation of office.

ACKNOWLEDGMENTS

A fair proportion of the first edition of *BluePrint for Investment* has survived in an updated form in this second edition. I would therefore like to repeat my thanks to those who read draft manuscripts of the first edition and offered criticism, suggestions and comment.

In preparing the second edition, I am grateful to Allen Truslove for his detailed comments and suggestions on early drafts of Chapter 8 which is entirely new. Mark Barsdell helped me find some of the data used in graphs and tables. Finally, I recognise that the manuscript benefited from the input of my colleagues at Mitchell & Co Pty Ltd.

However, in the end it must be recognised that unanimous agreement on investment matters is rare and the views expressed are mine.

Richard FitzHerbert
Melbourne
January 1998

Chapter 1

Introduction — Different Approaches to Investment Theory and Practice

THE NEED FOR INDEPENDENT JUDGEMENT

THESE DAYS, people who either own shares, get appointed as trustees, attend seminars or otherwise advertise their interest in investment matters, will soon find themselves receiving unsolicited material containing offers of assistance, 'research' opinions and newsletters.

In attempting to 'learn all about it', conscientious newcomers to the investment world may read circulars received from their 'adviser', subscribe to magazines, study books, attend seminars and/or develop an interest in the financial section of the daily newspaper. It will not be long before they are being bombarded with views and ideas from 'experts', without necessarily being conscious of it.

Most of the information investors read is a mixture of historical data, forecasts of the future and mere opinion. In most unknown fields it is often advisable to seek advice, but in the investment industry it is not so easy to distinguish between advice and promotional material, and between genuine advisers and people who have a vested interest in investors accepting their recommendations.

1

In their quest for sound advice, investors are, in a way, seeking ideas on how to make money which has few precedents in other fields in which professional advice is offered. Small business proprietors may seek professional legal, taxation or accounting advice, but working out how to make a profit is an entrepreneurial responsibility. Also, it is perhaps naive to think that someone who has unlocked the secrets of great wealth through investment will share these ideas for a few dollars per hour.

The larger broking firms have traditionally provided analysts' research reports to existing and prospective clients, but they cannot be expected to continue to provide this information free of charge to people who are likely to do their business elsewhere. In the days of fixed commissions it was not possible to save transaction costs, but market pressures and the emergence of 'discount brokers' may reduce the availability of relatively cheap research for non-institutional investors.

For investors who entrust their savings to professional investors, there is a second issue, apparent in the USA in 1997, of the paradox of experienced professionals admitting that their stock market is grossly overpriced, yet not being prepared to take any evasive action. There are two explanations for this phenomenon.

The first explanation is that the organisation operates on the stated intention of retaining a fixed proportion (sometimes 100%) of its funds invested in stocks and if their customers require this product then it is their responsibility to provide what the customer seeks.

The second explanation is that where a professional operates with discretion, history has demonstrated little sympathy for fund managers and other investment professionals who cause their clients to miss a stock market advance. On the other hand, if they remain more or less fully invested in a sharp decline, there has usually been grudging acceptance of the consequences.

An investor who relies on professionals may need to contend with an inflexible policy which overrides judgement. Alternatively, the professionals' business risk associated with selling too soon may prevent any action, no matter how high a market rises.

Consequently, investors can never rely exclusively on market professionals. They must be prepared to intervene, which requires that investors and trustees seek to develop their own independent standards of judgement.

One aspect of this process is knowing how to check and interpret the work of investment analysts. For example, there is no point in learning how to calculate a value indicator such as the price/earnings ratio without understanding its significance and limitations.

Consider, for example, an advertisement which appeared in 1992 in *Money Management*, a bi-monthly newspaper widely read by financial advisers and others in the 'managed funds' industry:[1]

"We would argue prospective 1992/93 price earnings ratios of 14x for industrial companies and 18x for resource companies are by no means demanding. ....

"At current levels we would strongly urge long-term investors to seek at least some exposure to the Australian equities market. This recommendation is based on the underlying fundamentals of the market, the likelihood of economic recovery and the likely returns offered by other asset classes.

"We believe that the outlook for investment in the property market, with the exception of the odd distressed sale, will prove to be relatively unrewarding over the next few years."

In many ways this sort of argument is repeated in industry newsletters, newspaper articles and brokers' recommendations. Alert and interested readers should consider a variety of questions which in this case would include the following:

(a) Did prospective price/earnings ratios of 14 and 18 respectively for industrial and mining companies indicate good buying opportunities?

(b) Are the calculations correct and what assumptions were used in performing them?

(c) Why is a higher price/earnings ratio acceptable for resource companies which operate in an industry generally accepted as being risky and having volatile share prices?

(d) Is it appropriate to use such a ratio to assess resource companies anyway?

(e) Was the strength of the positive sentiment expressed about the Australian equities market or the negative comments on property soundly based? Or did these opinions merely reflect the general market psychology of the time?

As events unfolded, this assessment turned out reasonably well over the following five years or so. Judging by published accumulation indices, investors in most Australian asset classes — including listed property trusts — fared reasonably well:

ACCUMULATION INDEX	JUNE 1992	JUNE 1997	% CHANGE
ASX All Industrials	9,950	21,241	+113%
ASX All Resources	2,853	5,093	+79%
ASX Property Trusts	5,720	11,014	+93%

However, having successfully backed the winner of the Melbourne Cup does not mean it would have been correct to have wagered a substantial sum in the first place.

Without the benefit of hindsight, assessing information for the purpose of making investment decisions is clearly not an easy task. Nevertheless the amateur investor or novice trustee should be encouraged to do so by the widespread (and almost universal) errors committed by well-educated, experienced, informed and well-paid investment professionals in the period leading up to the Australian stock market crash of October 1987.

Furthermore, the period leading up to the crash of 1987 demonstrates the importance of developing an ability to make independent assessments. Relying on the best advice and analysis the investment industry has to offer is not much use if the industry as a whole is out of step.

As we shall see, historical episodes demonstrate that it would be unwise to ignore the possibility that published opinions of almost all the operators in the investment industry as a whole can be simultaneously wrong — and by a wide margin at that.

It could be argued that it is impracticable for people who are not full-time participants in the securities industry to develop the essential capacity for independent judgement which was apparently lacking in the industry itself in the lead up to October 1987. This may well be an impossible task if the investor uses the same approach as the industry.

Let us therefore examine the various ways in which investment is approached at the present time — both in theory and practice — to see if the essential missing ingredients can be identified.

THE MODERN FINANCE THEORY APPROACH

One of the most important developments over the last 30 years has been the change in the way investment is taught in academic and other tertiary institutions from an 'old-fashioned' analytical approach to the 'modern mathematical' or econometric approach. This method of learning about different investments seeks to define various investment categories in terms of their risk and return characteristics.

A key assumption on which this mathematical approach is based is the premise that in capital markets there is keen competition between well-informed, rational and experienced professional investors, and as a result all securities are priced according to a formula under which return increases with risk. This 'formula' is widely known as the Capital Asset Pricing Model.

Markets which follow this formula are 'efficient' and 'risk' is measured in a mathematical way based on share price volatility. This risk coefficient is called 'beta'. According to this theory there is an optimum way of selecting securities to produce the greatest expected return for the minimum risk. Portfolios selected in this way are said to lie on the 'efficient frontier'.

To quote the editor of *The Australian Financial Review*, writing in 1991:[2]

"Today, investment as practised by the professional investors is a complex business, going beyond 'price/earnings ratios' and 'dividend yields' into kingdoms which are bounded by 'efficient frontiers', measured by 'benchmarks' and ruled by 'betas'. The experts now argue that the share market is an 'efficient market' and that a scientific approach based on mathematics and computers can be used to map the investment process."

If this view is correct then mathematics and computer models become important investment tools and there is no point in conducting traditional investment analysis. Thus the mathematician becomes important and the less mathematical analyst becomes an unnecessary expense.

In many academic institutions, particularly in the USA, reading lists have become dominated by texts which adopt this mathematical approach, with little exposure to material which questions the underlying assumptions.[3] In this process 'market efficiency' and the Capital Asset Pricing Model have become foundations of the educational approach rather than just one of a number of alternatives.

According to this theory, the excessive valuations and considerable risk of the Australian stock market in the months prior to October 1987 should not have been so large and should not have persisted for so long. To quote from the 1990 edition of *Investments* by Nobel laureate William Sharpe and his co-author:[4]

"... in an efficient market, a security's price will be a good estimate of its investment value, where investment value is the present value of the security's future prospects as estimated by well-informed and capable analysts. Any substantial disparity between price and value would reflect inefficiency. In a well-developed and free market, major inefficiencies are rare."

In a chapter entitled "Risk and Return" in the 1978 edition, William Sharpe wrote:[5]

"A security's beta with respect to the overall market is the single most important measure of its risk, as it measures the impact of the security on the risk of the overall market portfolio. And in an efficient market there is no free lunch: securities with little risk (low betas) can be expected to provide little reward (excess return)."

Indeed there has been a considerable danger that any students who entertain serious doubts about the efficient market hypothesis, would have trouble completing their courses. Many experienced professionals hold a completely different view including Warren Buffett, chairman of Berkshire Hathaway Inc., revered in the United States investment world for consistently outstanding results over several decades. In a book about Buffett, John Train wrote:[6]

> "[The efficient market hypothesis] has become so accepted in academia that, as Michael C. Jensen of the University of Rochester has said, we are dangerously close to the point where no graduate student would dare send off a paper criticising it. Nonetheless, many of the best investment practitioners, including Buffett, regard it as absurd."

Apart from Warren Buffett, an experienced Australian practitioner who has openly criticised the idea of market efficiency and the associated Capital Asset Pricing Model was Alan Geddes, former Managing Director of Mercantile Mutual Life, who had achieved excellent investment results for policy-holders over an extended period of years. In 1974, Geddes wrote:[7]

> "One David Goodstein, of New York, is reported to have written 'This econometric approach will put the old fashioned security analyst out of a job. What passes for security analysis today is in my opinion 150,000% bullshit.' David has been quoted for his colourful and enthusiastic language, although others might well award David's views an equally high percentage.

> "Even if it can be shown that in the past there has been some correlation between high volatility and high return (which I doubt), beta is still past history and to predict the future on this basis is hazardous. A sudden change in a company's affairs will alter its beta and make its past history irrelevant. No amount of playing mathematical games with alphas and betas can help find an undervalued security or one about to decline."

A third experienced practitioner is Austin Donnelly, well known thorn in the side of the financial planning industry. In *The Three R's of Investing*, Donnelly described the efficient market theory as the "the greatest fallacy of all". He went on to say:[8]

> "A generation of security analysts in some business schools have been trained in this serious fallacy."

However absurd some experienced and successful practitioners regard this mathematical or pseudo-scientific approach, it is so thoroughly entrenched in the investment intelligentsia that a serious text on the subject of investment principles cannot ignore this relatively recent educational approach.

As graduates of institutions teaching 'modern finance' have moved into the real world, so has the influence of the efficient market theory extended well beyond academia into investment institutions, regulatory thinking and professional bodies. For example, a book sponsored by the Association of Superannuation Funds of Australia in 1992 observed that:[9]

> *"One of the key connections all investors should make is the relationship between risk and return. Here the academics' models are supported by practical evidence from the market-place.* ....
>
> *"Most sensible people will only invest in risky assets if they stand a chance of ending up with a higher return. If the returns were not going to be any better regardless of the risk, everybody would only place their money in low-risk ventures."*

Unfortunately the events of October 1987 demonstrate that this 'simple logic' is far from the truth. Most of the mathematics associated with the Capital Asset Pricing Model and the efficient market theory is so sophisticated that it is difficult to challenge simply, but October 1987 provides one example of mathematical absurdity. When the stock market suddenly fell by 50% in October 1987, its volatility — as measured by past price fluctuations — had increased considerably. According to the theory the risk had therefore increased. **How could it possibly have been more risky to buy shares when the index stood at 1150 than one month earlier when the index stood at 2300?**

While sensible people will be risk-averse, the mathematical model assumes that investors are rational in their decisions. This is a comforting thought because the idea that boards of directors and investment committees controlling billions of dollars could be irrational in their decision-making is quite frightening.

As we will discuss a little later, it is quite possible for groups of rational and intelligent people to make irrational decisions under psychological pressure. This phenomenon was documented by Irving Janis in *Victims of Groupthink — a psychological study of foreign policy decisions and fiascos* published in 1972. It is also possible for business pressure to override judgment in fund management organisations — a conflict of interest discussed in Chapter 5.

Irrespective of the mathematical analyses, the efficient market theory treats risk and price volatility as one in the same thing and assumes that investors always make their decisions rationally. As we shall see in the remainder of this chapter, Austin Donnelly's observations (in *The Three R's of Investing* written prior to the 1987 crash) are far better supported by the historical record:[10]

> *"If all investment decisions were based on the objective assessment envisaged by the theory, then it may be somewhere close to the mark. But a lot of investment decisions are made because of the great enthusiasm of the moment, or because investors are persuaded by well-presented recommendations of a stock by brokers or investment advisers or by staff submissions to management of institutions."*

It is particularly interesting that since 1990 some of the US academics who had previously written papers and textbooks on 'modern portfolio theory' seem to be changing their mind. The 'flash of lightning on the road to Damascus' appears to have been a paper written by Eugene Fama and Ken French in 1992.[11] *Fortune* reported as follows:[12]

> *"In a paper that has been circulating recently in preliminary form and will be formally published this [US] summer, [Eugene] Fama and an associate, Kenneth R. French, also at [the University of] Chicago, studied the performance of more than 2,000 stocks from 1941 to 1990. Says French of their findings: 'What we are saying is that over the last 50 years, knowing the volatility of an equity doesn't tell you much about the stock's return.' Beta, say the boys from Chicago, is bogus."*

Or to put it bluntly, the sophisticated mathematics may be questionable as well as the assumption of rationality of investors and the confusion of risk with volatility.

The finding of Fama and French that there is little relationship between volatility and return will come as no surprise to followers of the Australian Stock Exchange Accumulation indices.

The better known ASX All Ordinaries index is divided into two groups of stocks — Resources and Industrials. These classifications are based on the principal business of the company and may differ from newspaper listings. For example, BHP is listed as an industrial stock in newspapers but forms part of the All Resources index. When these indices were introduced in 1980, accumulation indices were also established which allow for the reinvestment of dividends.

These indices have been published daily since December 1979 when they commenced with a value of 1000. Investors with any experience will know that resource stocks are more volatile than industrials and this is borne out in the calculations. But what about the return? The All Resources index is considerably more volatile[13] than the All Industrials so it should show a vastly superior return. Unfortunately the opposite is true as the table below demonstrates.

ASX Resources vs Industrials Volatility and Return 17 Years to December 1996

	ACCUMULATION INDEX 31.12.96	COMPOUND RETURN % p.a.	MONTHLY VOLATILITY %
ASX All Industrials	18,130	19.0	5.6
ASX All Resources	4,686	12.9	8.2

The immediate reaction to these figures by addicts of modern portfolio theory is almost invariably to try to find some new angle which leaves the assumed relationship between volatility and return intact. Some of the explanations have included:

(a) The results are not statistically significant (!)

(b) The Capital Asset Pricing Model has been misinterpreted

(c) The Capital Asset Pricing Model explains how investors expect the market to behave, not what actually happens

(d) The market in Australian resource stocks is dominated by foreign investors and resource stocks provide a useful hedge to international investors irrespective of their local volatility.

If this latter explanation is correct then the Capital Asset Pricing Model seems to be subject to the Coriolis effect — like bath water down the plug hole — it works one way in the Northern Hemisphere and the opposite way Down Under! More seriously, if resource stocks are permanently overpriced as a result of foreign investors, then why do Australian institutions, as a whole, tend to hold them at index weightings?

It is also interesting to note that, among all the reasons advanced for this phenomenon, the possibility that the Capital Asset Pricing Model might be suspect is rarely suggested.

Some critics of modern portfolio theory draw parallels with the old scientific ideas such as the notion that the sun revolves around the planet Earth. This theory created a long list of unexplained anomalies until it was suggested that planet Earth revolved about the sun.

These critics are trying to illustrate the point that instead of starting from a basic assumption of an 'efficient' market and making modifications for an increasing list of anomalies, one should start by assuming an inefficient market, recognising that efficiency may occur with perhaps the same frequency as a lunar eclipse.

One other possibility, under which academics can retain their efficient market and practitioners can justify their fees exploiting anomalies, is to change the definition of 'efficiency' in such a way that it accommodates both points of view. The quotation which follows comes from Fischer Black, a prominent academic in this field:[14]

> "... we might define an efficient market as one in which price is within a factor of 2 of value, i.e. the price is more than half of value and less than twice value. The factor of 2 is arbitrary, of course. Intuitively, though, it seems reasonable to me, in the light of sources of uncertainty about value and the strength of the forces tending to cause price to return to value. By this definition, I think almost all markets are efficient almost all of the time. 'Almost all' means at least 90%."

Maybe one day a group of professors of the 'efficient' persuasion will invest their own money during the one year in ten that prices exceed value by more than a factor of two — for example 1997 in the US? The true meaning of risk and the dangers of a pre-emptive assumption of market efficiency may then be learned by bitter experience.

CHARTING OR TECHNICAL ANALYSIS

The 'weak form' of the efficient market theory (also known as the random walk hypothesis) states that share price movements are independent of one another. Knowledge of past price movements is therefore of no value in predicting future price movements.

On the other hand, chartists or technical analysts argue that all relevant investment information about a share is reflected in its price and trading volume. Consequently, an investor can make money out of shares after learning how to interpret patterns on graphs to predict future price movements.

Many years ago charting was taken much more seriously than it is today. With the advent of newly available electronic equipment in the 1960s, university-based mathematicians tackled the claims of technical analysts with zeal.

Generally speaking the findings of academics contradicted most aspects of charting. In the last few years new methods of mathematical analysis and significantly cheaper and more powerful computers have enabled some patterns to be discovered, but not of sufficient magnitude to cover transaction expenses.[15] Studies over fairly long periods have established long-term patterns but these are not the sort of patterns which would be considered to be in the realm of chartists.

Nevertheless, technical analysis seems to be able to retain a semi-religious following. It seems strange that people who have unlocked the secrets of successful short-term speculation would bother to share their secrets with the public. Yet new books on technical analysis continue to appear in the bookshops — and glossy and expensive books at that.

If anyone has successfully used this knowledge to *consistently* make more money out of share trading than royalties received by writing books on the subject, their identity is unknown. Demolishing the claims of chartists was a useful achievement of academia. Unfortunately, the level of mathematical expertise required to understand the literature is beyond most people. In any event, experienced practitioners already knew that chart patterns had little predictive value before academia destroyed charting theories.

The crucial theoretical reason why charting is of no value is the independence of price movements in successive periods. It is perhaps ironic that this theory, having assisted in discrediting technical analysis, is now believed to be false.

However, in spite of recent discoveries of non-independent behaviour, option traders continue to use the 'Black-Scholes' model which was formulated more than 20 years ago. The continued acceptance of this model by practitioners, including those who put their own money on the line, suggests that the underlying assumption of independence is at least approximately correct.

THE VALUE–ORIENTED APPROACH

Prior to the advent of 'efficient market' theories, students of investment learnt about economics, balance sheets, profit and loss accounts and traditional 'ratio analysis'. A combination of economics, accounting and experience produced two different schools of thought which would both describe themselves as using 'fundamentals'.

One of these could be described as a 'growth' or 'forecasting' approach which pays particular attention to economies, industries and then individual companies and selecting areas where investment is assessed as being potentially lucrative. This forecasting approach is discussed in more detail later.

An alternative is to argue that growth forecasts and assessments of the economic outlook are unreliable. What really matters is making sure that any portfolio investments represent good value for money on a long-term basis and diversifying to ensure an 'average' result.

This value-oriented approach seeks to exploit differences between the price of individual securities and their value at the time. The continued success of this approach relies on the market being inefficient. The 'dean' of this particular faculty of thought was US author Benjamin Graham. In 1934 he wrote *Security Analysis* with David Dodd. Interestingly this book has been updated and reprinted five times, with slight changes in authorship. With each edition the basic principles are applied (more or less unchanged) to different circumstances. The latest edition appeared in mid-1987, 11 years after Graham's death.[16]

One of Graham's early students, Warren Buffett, gave a speech at Colombia University in 1984 to mark the 50th anniversary of the publication of *Security Analysis*.[17] This speech traced the excellent results which had been achieved over long periods of time by fund managers who had followed Graham's approach – 'The Superinvestors of Graham-and-Doddsville' as Buffett called them.

In his address, Buffett produced a number of tables which compared the investment results of the 'superinvestors' with the market average over comparable periods — in this case the Standard and Poors 500 share index. The normal yardstick used in these calculations is the average compound 'total return' which includes income and capital gains. A summary of these results is shown below.

Buffett went to some lengths to pre-empt criticism of his figures on theoretical grounds at the time. Compared to the typical investment performance table, these figures cover extended periods, changes in the people responsible for the results were not a consideration and the differences were both large and consistently so. Even if there are doubts about the figures or the applicability of such techniques in Australia, their sheer magnitude (relative to the market as a whole) would suggest that the 'value-oriented' approach is worthy of serious consideration.

The Superinvestors of Graham-and-Doddsville

FUND/ MANAGER	PERIOD	FUND RETURN % p.a.	S&P 500 RETURN % p.a.
Buffett Partnership	1957-69	23.8	7.4
Walter Schloss	1956-84	16.1	8.4
Tweedie Brown	1968-83	16.0	7.0
Sequoia Fund	1970-84	18.2	10.0
Charles Munger	1962-75	13.7	5.0
Pacific Partners	1965-83	23.6	7.0
Perlmeter Investments	1965-83	19.0	19.0
Average	17 years	18.6	7.5

Value-oriented investors use a number of yardsticks to evaluate 'value' such as dividend yields, price/earnings ratios and 'price/ net-assets' ratios. While they do not use these value indicators without careful evaluation, their portfolios would tend to include stocks whose value indicators were superior to market averages.

Numerous studies have been undertaken on the relationship between portfolios of stocks randomly selected on the basis of price/earnings ratios and subsequent investment returns. Almost without exception, these studies have indicated a strong correlation between this value indicator and subsequent results. Furthermore, the relationship between above average return and volatility seems, if anything, to be inverse.[18]

Traditional value indicators tend to be linked. Companies with relatively high dividend yields tend to have relatively low price/earnings and price/net-assets ratios. It is not surprising therefore that more recent studies, involving dividend yields and price/net-assets ratios, tend to confirm a strong relationship between portfolios randomly selected on the basis of either of these value indicators and subsequent stock market returns.[19]

In respect of price/net-assets ratios, the Australian Stock Exchange, in conjunction with the Frank Russell Co., have embarked on an interesting ongoing study by establishing style indices. Backdated to December 1990, they have divided the companies in the Australian All Ordinaries index into two groups based on the ratio of share price to net asset value. These ratios are recalculated each year and the groups reconstituted on the basis of the updated ratios. The group with the lower ratio contains the 'value' stocks and the higher ratio defines the 'growth' stocks.

Practitioners of the 'value' school would argue that there is more to value investing than calculating the ratio of market price to net tangible asset backing. They may also argue with the relatively short length of the study. However, they would not be particularly surprised with the results thus far.

The compound performance of the two groups over the six years ended December, 1996 was reported as follows:[20]

Performance of 'Growth' and 'Value' Stocks, 1990 to 1996

INDEX	COMPOUND RETURN % p.a.
ASX Russell 'Value'	19.9
ASX All Ordinaries	15.7
ASX Russell 'Growth'	10.3

In reporting these details, the editor recognised the significance of this study in the ongoing debate between value investors and efficient market theorists:

> *"For investors, the question must surely be: if the share market is efficient, why don't smart fund managers arbitrage away the out-performance by value stocks?"*

To which Warren Buffett has already replied:[21]

> *"I have seen no trend towards value investing in 35 years I've practised it".*

If the secret of value investing has been well known for so long, then why is it so ignored? In 1935, J.M. Keynes made the following comments in his famous *General Theory*:[22]

> *"It might have been supposed that competition between expert professionals, possessing judgement and knowledge beyond that of the ignorant individual investor, would correct the vagaries of the ignorant individual left to himself. It happens however, that the energies of the professional investor and speculator are, in fact, largely concerned, not with making superior long-term forecasts of the probable yield over its whole life, but with foreseeing changes in the conventional basis of valuation a short time ahead. They are concerned, not with what an investment is really worth...., but with what the market will value it at, under the influence of mass psychology, three months or a year hence."*

RELATIVE VALUE OR ABSOLUTE VALUE?

Value-oriented investors usually operate bottom-up — they invest their money in assets which meet their criteria and stop when they run out of ideas or money, whichever happens first. This approach would normally operate within diversification limits restricting the proportion to be held in any one security or industry.

Most of the results already quoted supporting the value-oriented approach relate to results obtained by portfolios selected on the basis of relative value. Yet, as we will see in the discussion of speculative booms, there are clearly times when investors should avoid the stock market altogether and, if already invested, consider at least a partial sale of their holdings.

It is very difficult for professional investors to pursue an absolute value approach in overpriced markets because of the risk to their business should an overheated market advance further. While it could be argued that professional investors who stay fully invested in overheated markets are speculating with the funds entrusted to their care, their clientele and industry commentators — with the genius bestowed by the gift of hindsight — may not see it that way.

A listed Australian investment company operating internationally made the 'mistake' of hedging its US portfolio in 1996, "because of its concerns about earnings growth and the attendant valuations of the US market".[23] The commentator in the financial press was unforgiving:[24]

> "The listed investment vehicle ... Platinum Capital Ltd, suffered a severe slump in profit in the six months ended last December, largely due to a *failure* to predict the extraordinary rise in the US share market."

Was this really a failure? Or were US investors, as a whole, becoming increasingly stupid? If US investors were not worried this optimism was not shared by a number of senior international monetary figures. According to a press report in late February 1997:[25]

> "A senior official of the International Monetary Fund yesterday endorsed concerns of the chairman of the US Federal Reserve, Dr Alan Greenspan, that US stock prices had risen too high and needed correction....

> "... price-earnings ratios in the US had risen way above the historic averages, and a 'gradual controlled decline' was desirable.

> "The concern is that the taller they rise, the harder they fall. It might not come down to where you want to go. There might be an overreaction."

History will no doubt have its say in due course. For the record it might be worth noting that the Standard and Poors 500 index stood at around 800 points when this comment was made. In the meantime the pressure on professional 'value investors' to remain more or less fully invested should be recognised. Investors wishing to pursue a policy of absolute value will therefore need to be prepared to take overriding evasive action in overheated markets.

THE FORECASTING APPROACH

The idea behind the forecasting approach is to analyse the state of the world economy, political events and anything else considered relevant to decide where best to invest. For example investors may decide that the outlook for property is particularly depressing. As a result new investment funds will be directed elsewhere and investors may go further and seek to sell some property assets to divert the funds into a more promising arena.

By way of contrast with value-oriented investors, forecasters usually operate top-down. They first decide what proportions of their funds are going to be invested in property, industrial shares, mining shares, overseas or in fixed-interest securities. Once this decision is complete further categorisation may take place (for example the industrial share component may be broken down into industry classifications) before individual securities are selected.

While forecasters usually operate top-down, the converse is not necessarily correct. The top-down approach, under which proportions of an investment portfolio are first allocated to various asset classes, may be based on either value-oriented or forecasting lines.

While there is a considerable amount of logic to the forecasting approach, obtaining forecasts which are sufficiently reliable to enable the investor to act and which become available while the forecast is not already reflected in the market is almost impossible because some of the best brains in the world are committed to this task.

Professional fund management organisations and financial institutions invariably claim to operate on fundamental lines although it is sometimes difficult to understand the technical jargon with which their investment policy is described. For example, a presentation brochure of the fund management subsidiary of a major bank dated September 1988 said:[26]

"Prime emphasis is placed on asset allocation, based on economic and corporate analysis leading to projected sectoral rates of return. It is our experience that careful asset mix selection in the first instance is the most important factor in providing the framework which leads to superior returns and to better results from individual investment decisions."

The jargon is a little heavy, but it seems to describe a top-down approach. It appears that at the highest level decisions are based on forecasts rather than value-based assessments but this is not clear.

Interestingly, this organisation also claimed to use 'modern mathematical' methods in its decision-making process. The following passage will no doubt make sense to students of the efficient market but those who had trouble understanding the above quotation will see that their ignorance was punished lightly.

"Our attitude to risk is very clear. We control risk to an acceptable level where we achieve appropriate increases in return and have invested considerable time, money, and effort in computer models to determine efficient risk frontiers. If in our calculations an increase in risk profile will only result in a small increase in return, we will move back down the risk profile."

One hopes that those responsible for individual decisions at a lower management level understood what they were supposed to be doing.

Learning about investment from a fundamental approach is hard going. Apart from anything else it takes time to learn the language in which investment topics are discussed before attention can be devoted to the calculation of dividend yields, price/earnings ratios and so on. Serious investors will need to learn how to do this, but first they will need to be convinced that the effort is worthwhile.

On the other hand, if the market is 'efficient' then there is no benefit to be gained by doing such calculations, so convincing readers that 'efficiency' is an idea of dubious validity is an essential prerequisite.

PERFORMANCE CHASING

In the last 20 years, investment performance tables have become an important part of the investment scene. Good performance attracts both publicity and business to professional fund management organisations while bad performance leads to 'please explain' requests if not contract termination. Regular features of the 'performance' of fund management organisations and their products are regularly published in newspapers and specialist magazines.

There is perhaps some intuitive logic in the suggestion that a fund manager or investment product at the top of the table will do better in the future than one at the bottom of the table in much the same way that a football team at the top of its division should be expected to defeat a team at the bottom.

A brochure printed after the 1987 crash by an Australian life insurance company contained the following advice:[27]

"There are many different fund managers, including merchant banks, sharebrokers and insurance companies, and many of these offer a wide range of funds.

"Faced with such a bewildering array of 'managed investments', the decision may well come down to the basis of 'which is the best managed?'

"Unfortunately this question cannot be answered with 100 per cent certainty. But the degree of uncertainty can be reduced by examining and comparing the respective performances of individual investment managers.

"The most common way of doing this is by comparing their past rates of return. This can be done by analysing investment surveys regularly published by specialists in this field."

But is the intuitive logic of using investment performance tables to select a 'managed fund' any use? If, as is usually the case with football, there is a large skill difference between teams at opposite ends of the league table, then performance chasing would be quite sound.

There are a number of difficulties in using past data to evaluate the present management team, such as changes in personnel and investment process. But, in addition to these qualitative factors, the differences in the investment performance league table could be due to luck as much as judgement and expertise.

So, do performance tables show the effects of chance or superior management and expertise? This is one investment topic where classical mathematics is quite useful. There are a number of standard statistical tests which can be used to decide the matter in much the same way that it would be possible to decide whether there was any truth in a claim to be able to consistently win a coin-flipping competition.

Generally speaking, statistical tests of the proposition that good investment performance in one period justifies the expectation that this will continue have proved negative and experts in the field seem to accept this conclusion.[28] A paper presented to the Institute of Actuaries of Australia in 1989 observed that:[29]

> "While [investment performance league tables] are attractive from a public relations point of view they are generally agreed to have little or no statistical significance."

It is perhaps not surprising that published investment performance league tables usually contain a 'health' warning:

> "....these past returns should not be used in isolation to assess likely future results."

The concept of statistical significance (or lack thereof) may not be familiar to non-mathematicians, but those who do understand the concept will realise that if performance differences are not statistically significant, then the 'health' warning may deserve more emphasis.

The investing public seems to be heavily influenced by performance. Financial institutions seem to find 'performance' advertising an effective method of attracting business.

Consider, for example, a full page newspaper advertisement a few weeks before the Australian stock market crash of 1987.[30] The narrative contained the following statements:

"If only....

How many investors are kicking themselves for not getting in on the ground floor when the XYZ Equity Trust was launched last year?

They missed out on an excellent return in just the first 10 months that the Trust has operated.

But the good news is you can still invest in this Trust and, in addition, XYZ has launched two new Equity Trusts. ...

Keen investors will not want to miss out on these opportunities and, of course, the XYZ Property Trust is also well worth consideration.

For a copy of the Prospectus ...

XYZ Equity Trust 100.6%* return in first 10 months.

The organisation which placed the advertisement, was a subsidiary of an internationally prestigious financial institution. At the top of the advertisement there was a young man sitting in front of a computer screen on which was displayed "100.6%*".

At the bottom of the advertisement the following statement appeared in smaller print:

"*The future performance of the XYZ Equity Trust may be different from this rate."

It was!

THE GROUPTHINK FACTOR

It seems to be well accepted that 'performance' has an important influence on the investing habits of the public, superannuation fund trustees and their professional advisers.

As 'performance' is so important in determining the destiny of vast quantities of investment funds, it becomes necessary for financial institutions and fund management organisations to 'perform' to generate business — an orientation that percolates through everyone involved with investment decision-making.

Given this orientation, clearly enunciated, the average investor may be surprised to learn that, in general, this eagerly sought 'performance' does not eventuate.

Following the success of statistical analysis over charting theories, which now seems suspect, university-based academics turned their computing firepower on the US mutual fund industry. Numerous investigations were conducted into its performance which concluded that as a whole the industry did no better than market averages and there were very few organisations which persistently 'outperformed' the averages.

In academia, this observation and a number of similar observations such as the inaccuracies of brokers' earnings forecasts, led to the idea of 'market efficiency' discussed earlier.

However 'efficiency' is but one of a number of possible explanations for the academics' observations.

For example, one possible explanation as to why mutual fund performance is no better than average is that these funds are so large that it is impossible for them to take advantage of market anomalies without affecting the market so much that the anomalies they were seeking to exploit would disappear.

Unfortunately neither of these suggestions explain why speculative orgies emerge from time to time in which people who should know better become deeply involved. In an earlier book on stock market psychology, David Dreman of 'Contrarian Investing' fame proposed an alternative thesis based on the phenomenon of 'groupthink'.[31]

This term is generally attributed to Irving Janis, professor of psychology at Yale University as a result of his analysis of US foreign policy fiascos.[32] Janis defined 'groupthink' as a:

"... mode of thinking that people engage in when they are deeply involved in a cohesive in-group, when the members, striving for unanimity, override their motivation to realistically appraise alternative courses of action."

Leon Mann, professor of organisational behaviour at Melbourne University, is reported to have suggested that many of the problems of the 1980s were due to 'groupthink'.[33] The report described this phenomenon as:

*"... a **characteristic of group** behaviour that allows otherwise intelligent people to commit themselves to foolish action."*

Professor Mann was probably not thinking of the stock market, but the problems were related. However, Dreman argued that professional investors are all part of a psychological crowd caused in part by the pressure to perform and the nature of the business. As part of such a group it is not unusual for otherwise rational people to behave in an irrational way. They react emotionally, they ignore opinions which contradict the prevailing market mood, and people who express such opinions are treated as outcasts. The reason that professional investors fail to beat the averages and periodically make monumental errors of judgement is often the result of this psychological pressure. More recently there is the additional psychological reinforcement of this phenomenon caused by the financial pressure to 'perform'.

There is little doubt that psychology is an important factor in capital markets. However, if Dreman's groupthink thesis is correct then performance figures, as well as being statistically insignificant (and therefore of limited use), may reinforce speculative trends and exacerbate declines. The regular publication of investment performance surveys creates a great deal of pressure. It is quite possible that this pressure created a favourable environment for groupthink, and in consequence the publication of performance surveys was a partial cause of the Australian stock market bubble of 1987.

Ten years later, in 1997, it seems that the popularity of US mutual funds is based on past performance, partially at least. The next few years may provide shed some light on the validity of the hypothesis that the publication of investment performance data and its consequential public following reinforces speculative trends and exacerbates declines.

HISTORY — THE ESSENTIAL SUBSTITUTE FOR EXPERIENCE

The average investor or trustee usually achieves this status quite late in life. The time required to acquire sufficient experience before making decisions on investment matters needs to be measured in decades rather than years. To some extent this experience can be obtained indirectly by studying relevant history.

As far as the average retiree is concerned there are no second chances. It is too late to discover at the age of 80, that investment decisions taken at age 65 were unsound. On the other hand, a superannuation fund trustee may only serve for 10 years before being seconded to another position.

It is fairly essential, therefore, that the average non-professional investor acquire experience in a second hand fashion by studying historical investment episodes.

People who have worked in the industry for 20 years or so will have learnt a great deal from day-to-day experience. But the events of 1987, the Tokyo bubble of 1989, the bargains of the mid-1970s and the overvaluations of Wall Street in 1997 do not occur frequently. Experienced professionals would also benefit from this historical knowledge just in case similar discrepancies between price and value on such a grand scale recur in their lifetime.

In a foreword to the 1975 edition of his history of the 1929 Wall Street crash, J.K. Galbraith wrote:[34]

"As a protection against financial illusion or insanity, memory is far better than law. When the memory of the 1929 disaster failed, law and regulation no longer sufficed. For protecting people from the cupidity of others and their own, history is highly utilitarian. It sustains memory and memory serves the same purpose as the [Securities and Exchange Commission] and, on the record, is far more effective."

Most people reading about the 1929 Wall Street crash would find it hard to believe that it could ever happen again. Since that time there have been a number of minor speculative episodes of one sort or another such as the 'wool boom' of the early 1950s, the 'Poseidon boom' of 1970, the 'nifty fifty' era of the late 1970s, the 'gold boom' of 1980 or the Hunt brothers' 'silver squeeze' of 1981. These episodes have usually been confined to one commodity or a section of a market and were fairly small compared to Wall Street in 1929.

However, several decades after the Wall Street crash of 1929 two speculative binges of similar size were to grip international stock markets. This dubious honour was first achieved by the Japanese stock market, which at its peak in late 1989 represented 50% of the capitalisation of all world stock exchanges. The second honour goes to Wall Street in 1997 where valuations may have reached 1929 levels.

An investment historian would have readily recognised the Australian stock market of 1986/87 and the Japanese market a few years later for what they were — manifestations of a herd of well-educated (and well-paid) bankers, brokers, advisers and fund managers suffering from temporary insanity — caused perhaps by 'performance myopia'. There were some exceptions, but their influence was small and their counsel was generally ignored.

An interesting example relevant to Wall Street in 1997 was the comment of the chairman of the Federal Reserve on its *"irrational exuberance"*. The first time he made this comment it had an immediate effect for a few days, but was then forgotten.

It seems impossible for people to invest their own money with safety, or to accept the position of trustee of a superannuation scheme unless they are equipped to assess the advice they receive, or the general investment attitudes of the time, against the historical record. These booms (and the subsequent busts) generally represented extraordinarily good opportunities for those who were not seduced by the investment fashions of the time. History is an important defence against crowd psychology, to say nothing of advice which espouses the conventional wisdom of the day.

Peter Lynch, the highly successful manager of the Fidelity Magellan Fund, reflected on his own education as follows:[35]

"In college ... I avoided science, math, and accounting – all the normal preparations for business. I was on the arts side ...

"As I look back on it now, it's obvious that studying history and philosophy was much better preparation for the stock market than, say, studying statistics. Investing in stocks is an art, not a science, and people who've been trained to rigidly quantify everything have a big disadvantage. All the math you need in the stock market ... you get in fourth grade."

The technical jargon, (and in some cases the mathematics) which appears in some texts on the subject of investment is daunting. This is perhaps unfortunate because much of it is not really needed.

In 50 or so years' time, the investment historian may note that the current pre-occupation with 'betas', 'efficient frontiers' and other aspects of the 'capital asset pricing model' proved to be as transient as technical analysis.

Books on charting, get-rich-quick trading, and modern portfolio theory will continue to appear and be read by people who know no better. The only investment approach which seems to have worn the test of time is the fundamental value-oriented approach. This is perhaps an important lesson of history. It is confirmed by studying the methods used by outstanding investors.

LESSONS OF THE MASTER ARTISTS

If, as suggested by Peter Lynch, and countless other practitioners, investment is more of an art than a science, we should, like art students, study the methods of the master craftsmen.

Money managers have proved to be an interesting group of people in the public's eye, and a number of authors have published biographical studies. It did not take long for enquiring minds, such as John Train, to try to identify the attributes of those who were consistently successful.

In 1980, Train wrote a qualitative account of the methods employed by a number of individuals whose investment results over extended periods of years were outstanding.[36] He repeated the exercise in 1989[37] and, in between, devoted one book to Warren Buffett, the most outstanding student of Benjamin Graham.[38]

It was interesting to study <u>Train's conclusions</u>, largely based on qualitative analysis and observation of the masters' approaches to investment. It was obvious that his research was far from superficial, and he identified three methods which seemed to work:[39]

> *"There are basically three ways to do unusually well in the stock market:*
>
> 1. *Buy stocks that are cheap and sell them when they are reasonably priced: value investing.*
> 2. *Buy into companies that will grow and grow and grow and stay along for the ride.*
> 3. *Discover a whole new investment area."*

and some which did not: [40]

> *"None of the masters in this book relies on the tools so beloved of pundits: regression analysis, modern portfolio theory, industry overweightings and underweightings, technical analysis, or higher math."*

The growth stock approach is not discussed here because the size of such companies in Australia usually makes them privately owned. Identifying stocks which have grown rapidly in the past is relatively easy. Finding companies which are about to embark on a period of substantial growth before the company's prospects are reflected in the market price is extremely difficult.

When 'growth' stocks have already been recognised as such in the market place there is a danger that they have become 'hope' stocks. To quote Geddes in *Investment in a Changing World:*[41]

> *"The so-called growth stocks are stocks which have grown in the past and which optimists assume will grow in the future. Because they are*

bought in large quantities by institutions, trustees, charities, overseas investors and others who know no better their prices are always too high."

Consequently the three potentially successful approaches identified by Train are stated in order of difficulty. The idea of discovering a whole new investment area or an undiscovered 'growth stock' may appeal to the pioneering spirit but investors who attempt either of these activities without the skills which would also enable them to benefit from value investing are unlikely to succeed.

Chapter 2

The Lessons of History

BUBBLES, BUST AND FASHIONS

A PHENOMENON of some significance to investors is the tendency of some capital market participants to periodically indulge in speculative orgies of considerable dimensions. The historical record suggests that during a boom or the subsequent bust most of those who are relied upon to take appropriate action or provide timely advice fail to do so. An interesting phenomenon in recent years is the publication of clues which are readily accessible to a conscientious reader of ordinary newspapers.

It is plausible that 'groupthink' is a major contributing factor in all of these manias. More important, from the point of view of the investor, is their continued recurrence. This reinforces the importance of learning to exercise independent judgement.

The preoccupation with performance prior to the crash of 1987 and how it was succeeded with an interest in risk-aversion immediately afterwards was recalled by two actuaries employed by a major Australian mutual life office at the time:[1]

"... the main criterion to judge good performance was how big the last quarterly return was... Since the October 1987 stock market crash, the ball game has changed and risk is now something to be considered."

It is interesting how risk suddenly became important after it had been reduced by a 50% decline in market prices. It seems irrational that trustees should be worrying about risk after the crash if they were not worrying about it before — unless they now recognise that they were wrong to ignore risk before the crash. (Were they not victims of groupthink?)

It is easy to identify such episodes with the benefit of hindsight but it has proved very much more difficult for those involved at the time to stand aloof and conduct their financial affairs accordingly.

Conscientious trustees and/or investors may therefore regard the task of identifying occasions when capital markets are behaving irrationally as beyond their field of expertise and seek to delegate this decision by engaging professionals, directly or indirectly. Private investors only have themselves to blame if this does not work; but trustees may need to consider whether not trying to identify irrational professional behaviour constitutes abdication of responsibility rather than delegation.

Although the classification is somewhat subjective, historical episodes of interest in this context can be divided into events of wide historical interest such as the Wall Street crash of 1929 which ushered in the Great Depression, and more isolated events such as the speculation in Surfers Paradise real estate in the early 1980s.

Major events involving important markets usually interest economic historians. The documentary material is thorough and, if the reader can ignore the plight of those who were ruined, 'ripping good yarns'. The events in this category would include the Dutch Tulipomania around 1635, the fortunes of the South Sea Company in London in 1720, the Mississippi company in Paris at around the same time and the Wall Street crash of 1929.

The Japanese stock market of 1989 and the Australian 'entrepreneurial' era of the mid 1980s may also fall into this category when today's historians are looking for suitable material in a few years time.

Such historically significant events do not happen frequently. However other bubbles (and busts) in individual stocks, industries or national stock markets are quite common. Anyone who is able to identify lesser bubbles should find it relatively easy to identify a bubble of international or historical significance.

Writing in *Two Centuries of Panic*,[2] Trevor Sykes had no trouble identifying enough material to compile an extensive and tightly-written history of corporate crashes in Australia alone.

While the bubbles and busts in Australia in the last 25 years have not reached the significance of the 1929 Wall Street crash, the last 25 years have seen a number of events which had a significant effect on the Australian economy as a whole or individual industries. These would include the following:

(a) The 'Poseidon' boom of 1969/70

(b) The gold futures boom of 1979/80

(c) Surfers Paradise real estate in the early 1980s

(d) Ostrich farming in the early 1990s.

Bubbles and busts of similar significance occurred elsewhere. For example the US stock market began the 1960s with a fascination for electronics which perhaps can be illustrated by the price of shares in International Business Machines. IBM had achieved an outstanding corporate record which the stock market had embraced with perhaps a little too much exuberance.[3] The shares traded on a price/earnings ratio of 50 and a dividend yield of 1% (not unlike Japanese shares as a whole at their peak in 1989).

In the early 1970s Wall Street developed into a two-tier market in which some favoured large companies — colloquially known as the 'nifty-fifty' — traded at price/earnings ratios of 80. The sudden increase in the price of oil exposed some fundamental weaknesses and US citizens also became obsessed with the Watergate scandal. The 'nifty-fifty' fell by 80% in 1974 when Wall Street fell sharply. As Alan Geddes commented:[4]

"The loss when a blue chip becomes a blue duck is severe."

While a study of these bubbles will help identify the symptoms in similar future situations, it is interesting to note the positive attitude of experienced value-trained investors in the troughs which followed. For example, after the collapse of the 'nifty-fifty' in 1974, the (now) legendary Warren Buffett was asked in an interview with *Forbes* magazine, how he felt. Buffett replied:[5]

"Like an oversexed guy in a whorehouse. This is the time to start investing."

The next major low in US stocks occurred in the early 1980s when the Dow Jones Industrial Average was trading at roughly the same level that had been reached 20 years earlier, but higher than the trough of 1974. US investors were pessimistic about their economy and the world in general. Although dividends were more or less maintained, corporate profitability was very low.

In discussing the US stock market of 1982 in *The New Contrarian Investment Strategy*, David Dreman concluded:

> *"When I was a student reading the newspapers of the 1930s, 1940s, and 1950s, I was amazed by the value so abundant in the stock markets of those days and felt a little cheated because I thought the great days of investment coups all lay in the past.*
>
> *"Today, nothing seems further from the truth. Institutional concentration, conformity pressures on professionals, and overreactions to the current economic problems seem to me to present the investor with some of the greatest stock market opportunities in decades."*

From its low in 1982, Wall Street recovered gradually. Even at the low point reached after the crash of 1987, the Dow was still roughly double its 1982 level.

THE POSEIDON BOOM

Let us begin this selective look at some recent bubbles with a very brief summary of a mania which will be permanently etched in the memory of Australians born before 1950. An excellent account of the madness of this period appears in *The Money Miners*, by Trevor Sykes.[6] Apparently Sykes shares Galbraith's view on the importance of history in preparing people for the next:[7]

> *"A quarter of a century has passed since the great nickel boom of 1969-70. It must still rank as the wildest boom in Australia's history. In the space of four months, a small, obscure Adelaide-based stock ran from 80¢ to $280 a share and dragged the entire rag-tag and bobtail speculative share market into the sky in its wake.*
>
> *"... [This book is] written in the hope that if the Australian public understands what happened in 1969-70 they will be better prepared for the next boom.*
>
> *"Because there will certainly be another."*

In the late 1960s mining shares were eagerly sought, so much so that companies emphasised their mining interests in their annual reports in much the same way as they feature their environmental policies today. In 1970 a company could almost be certain of significantly increasing its share price by announcing the establishment of a mining or exploration division.

It all started fairly rationally. Broken Hill Proprietary had discovered significant quantities of oil in Bass Strait and in 1967 Western Mining had brought the Kambalda nickel mine into production in a little over one and a half years since discovery of the ore-body. At the time, miners at the principal suppliers of nickel were on strike and the price of nickel had soared. The country was gripped with nickel fever.

The star of the show was an Adelaide-based mineral exploration company — Poseidon NL — whose 25 cent shares rose from 2 cents in 1966 to $281 in February 1970. At this price it was capitalised at three times the capitalisation of Westpac (then the Bank of New South Wales) and approximately 30% of the capitalisation of Broken Hill Proprietary.[8] Mining the ore-body which had caterpulted the company to fame was beset with problems and Poseidon was delisted in 1976. It was resuscitated as a gold mining company in the 1980 gold boom but that is another story.

The mining boom collapsed in 1970, but it had disguised a fairly buoyant market in industrial shares as well. In November 1972, the Australian Labor Party won government after 20 odd years in the cold. They pursued their policies with considerable zeal and may have tried to do too much too quickly. As a result, inflationary pressures looked like getting out of control and a fierce credit squeeze was imposed in mid-1974. Unfortunately, this coincided with an international economy trying to cope with a sudden increase in the price of oil, a US market pre-occupied with Watergate and a British economy struggling with its own political and economic problems. The Australian All Ordinaries fell by 50% in a couple of months.

$US 300 BILLION BUILDING SOCIETY DISASTER OF THE 1980s

While the crash of the US stock market in October 1987 was unprecedented in its speed, the crisis of the Savings and Loans Associations may have been more important to the US economy as a whole — in a way similar to some of the problems which emerged in some Australian institutions in the early 1990s.

Savings and Loans Associations or 'thrifts' — the US equivalent of building societies — pay a premium to a federal agency to 'insure' their deposits against failure of their 'thrift'. The insurance of deposits combined with a relaxation of laws governing the investments of Savings and Loans Associations proved to be an explosive mixture. The relaxed investment regulations which became law in 1982 enabled thrifts to undertake quite speculative loans without submitting to the discipline of the market.

Without deposit insurance such activities would risk a 'run' on the organisation, but with their deposits insured, depositors showed little concern. The only problem was that the losses became so huge it was beyond the financial ability of the guarantee fund to shore up defaults.

In their introduction to their chronicle of the US Savings and Loans disaster, Stephen Pizzo and his co-authors wrote:[9]

> *"We believed we were in a race to identify the players in this massive looting operation. In the process we uncovered mobsters, arms dealers, drug money launderers, and the most amazing and unlikely cast of wheeler-dealers that ever prowled the halls of financial institutions. The damage they did to this country's thrift industry will be with us well into the next century. It will significantly add to our national debt and will cost every taxpayer another $2,000 in taxes over the next ten years. The 150-year-old thrift industry itself may not survive."*

Luckily for US Savings and Loans depositors, the US Federal Government decided to bail out the industry at a massive cost to other taxpayers — but in many cases the blind acceptance of an insolvent guarantor, and speculative acceptance of an eventual government rescue was cynically exploited by some very unscrupulous people.

Interestingly, a report on the Australian Financial System in 1997 (the Wallis Report), commissioned by the Australian government, apparently flirted with the idea of deposit insurance for Australian banks.

TULIPS, GOLD FUTURES AND OSTRICHES

Gambling seems to be a genetic disease of homo sapiens which lurks just below the surface. In favourable conditions it will break out and spread like measles. The arguments of this chapter suggest that a study of history is an effective inoculation.

The curious speculation in tulip bulbs in 17th century Holland may seem a little remote from the purchase of ordinary shares 350 years later, but human genetics has not changed much in the interim.

Tulips arrived in England around 1600 and in Holland some years earlier. By degrees it gradually became fashionable to collect them and their prices began to soar. According to Charles Mackay in his *Memoirs*, first published in 1841:[10]

> *In 1634, the rage among the Dutch to possess [tulips] was so great that the ordinary industry of the country was neglected, and the population, even to its lowest dregs, embarked on the tulip trade."*

Early in 1636, someone offered 12 acres of land for one root of the prized *Semper Augustus*. Exchanges were established for trading tulips in Amsterdam, Rotterdam and numerous other towns. An English visitor spent some months in gaol for mistakenly eating a tulip bulb believing it to be an onion. People sold their houses to trade in tulips.

When the bubble burst, there were large public meetings and a large deputation was sent to Amsterdam to lobby the government to find a solution. Bankruptcies and defaults on contracts to purchase tulips became widespread although a court subsequently ruled that such debts were debts incurred in gambling on credit and in consequence unenforceable at law. The disruption to the economy was so great that it did not return to normal for many years.[11]

Gold and silver seem to have had a fascination which has captivated people at many times in history. Perhaps this fascination is enhanced because governments periodically forbid their citizens to buy gold to protect currencies which they have debased.

In the mid-1970s when 3½% War Loan, an irredeemable British government security, was trading on a yield in excess of 15% (and whose price had therefore fallen to approximately 20% of its original face value – to say nothing of the loss of purchasing power) a journalist is reported to have remarked:

> *"The Chancellor of the Exchequer has said that gold is only useful for filling teeth and hanging on womens' necks. Perhaps he should advise to what purpose one might put government bonds!"*

In the 1970s, the prohibition on purchase of gold bullion by private citizens was relaxed in many countries and trading in gold futures contracts was introduced on the New York Commodities Exchange (Comex). Under the Comex contract the purchaser undertakes to take delivery and the seller undertakes to deliver 100 ounces of gold at an agreed price on a specified date.

In practice very few futures contracts are settled by delivery. The purchaser pays a deposit and if the price quoted on the futures exchange moves against him he is required to pay a margin call equal to the unrealised loss. Subject to the same requirements for paying deposits and maintaining margins a speculator can also sell short in the expectation of profiting from a price decline. A clearing house is interposed between all buyers and sellers enabling both parties to independently 'close out' their contracts prior to delivery.

The net effect of futures contracts is incredible leverage. A speculator can enter a short or long position for a contract with a full face value of $35,000 with a deposit in the order of $1,000.

In Sydney a futures exchange had existed for some years trading in wool contracts. A contract in live cattle had also been introduced but it was not active. However this was all but forgotten when a 50 ounce gold contract was introduced in 1978. Futures trading exploded. Wool traders became instant experts on gold. Struggling futures brokers with a handful of staff expanded by a factor of 10 and became highly profitable.

In January 1980, the price of gold rose to $US 850 per ounce. The price of the Sydney gold contract rose $50 in one day because a Soviet warship was spotted in the Indian Ocean. The premium on forward delivery had risen so high in Sydney that Australian arbitragers were able to purchase Comex contracts overnight and sell Sydney contracts the following morning at a differential of $100 per ounce. This differential was so large it was hardly worth bothering to cover the exchange risk.

This episode produced its usual array of experts on gold prices including the very interesting *Aden Gold Study*.[12] The third printing of this 30-page study appears to have been published in late 1981 when the price of gold had fallen to approximately $US 400 per ounce. The preface claimed that the authors' research:

"spans 15 years of data and has resulted in the development of many new systems that incorporate the best of fundamental, technical, cyclical and mathematical analysis."

In concluding their study the authors bravely attempted to forecast gold price movements:

"Although the next cyclical peak appears to be about five years away, the approximate timing and price levels can be estimated using the regularities in the gold cycle.

"We can expect that for the first two years of the bull market the price will be in a steady but quiet uptrend. In early to mid-1984, gold will probably be reaching its old high of $850; by this time there will be rising inflation, interest rates and oil prices. Soon after gold rises above $850, price movements will become much more dramatic and will continue until gold reaches its first price peak. Gold timing tools indicate that this peak will occur between September, 1985 and September 1986 ...

Knowing the timing of the peak was very helpful but what was really required was the projected price. The authors obliged:

"Figuring a 340% increase from the $850 level for the next cyclical peak, we arrive at a price of about $3,750. Technical analysis indicates that the price will peak within the approximate price range of $3,750 to $4,900."

To date (November 1997), the price of gold has yet to return to its 1980 peak and was approximately $US 300 at the time of writing.

A more sober assessment, which is also relevant to the next story, appeared in *Metals Week* a few months prior to the peak. At this time the price was $US 440 per ounce and the possibility of '$5,000 gold' was being canvassed. *Metals Week* commented:[13]

"Production costs in the US are between $150 and $200 per oz; in South Africa they're somewhat lower. In a rational world gold would be bought by people who use it, and they would pay a price that would cover production costs and allow the producer to make a reasonable profit.

"But this is not a rational world. The price of gold today is being moved by uncertainties, fears, and dreams...

"In the history of the world there has never been a dream that didn't end. And in the history of the world there has never a speculative binge that didn't end too."

An interesting bubble in the early 1990s was ostrich farming. This activity was not new to Australia. Approximately 100 birds were imported from South Africa in the 1880s. Imports were effectively stopped a few years later when the South African government imposed heavy export taxes as a reaction to Australian success in exporting plumes to England. The feather industry collapsed after World War I and the birds were apparently let loose or sold to zoos.

According to an article in *The Echo* (Geelong) on 26 August 1992 the Australian ostrich population had reached 6,000 to 8,000 birds (presumably achieved by recapturing and breeding from feral animals) and farming was still in a stocking stage but *"with each breeding pair producing 40 chicks or more a year, slaughtering is scheduled to commence in 1996"*.[14] At this time a fully grown bird was expected to fetch $700 of which the hide and meat are the principal components.

What was surprising was the price of breeding stock. In 1989, a rural newspaper carried a report of an ostrich auction sale attended by 500 people in Narrandera NSW.[15] Prior to the auction the gathering was addressed by an agricultural counsellor from South Africa who warned:

"The ostrich business is, like the bird, unpredictable at best."

These warnings did not seem to dent the enthusiasm of the crowd. There was much excitement when the first bird brought a price which was almost twice experts' prior expectations, which were themselves considered too optimistic by the vendor. The report continued:

"Even the auctioneer ... looked a trifle stunned.

"Lot three topped the ladder when a 21-month-old female made $52,000 ...

"After the dust had settled, more than $850,000 had changed hands for 45 ostriches offered."

It is perhaps not surprising that the ostrich advertisements in *The Weekly Times* took up three quarters of a page in 1992. In September 1992, one advertisement offered a pair of 3½ year old *"proven"* adult breeders for $120,000.[16] Other advertisements offered ostrich insurance with *"Premium Financing Available"* and ostrich transport with *"on board monitor to protect your investment"*. Considering the prices of these animals it was not surprising that most of them were *"microchipped"*.

There did seem to be some madness in paying around $50,000 for an animal which had a slaughter value of the order of 1% of this amount and which could produce 40 chicks a year per breeding pair. But these animals were not being bought to generate consumable produce. They were being purchased for breeding birds which could also be sold for breeding.

At 1992 prices the birds were too valuable for slaughter. The specialist ostrich magazine carried a report which demonstrated the severe shortage in ostrich meat:[17]

> *"At the request of some enthusiastic ostrich breeders, [the head chef of Huntingale Golf Club] has developed the following recipes for us. He intends to develop more recipes however he needs more meat for experimentation, so please do not hesitate to call him if you have any available."*

At the prices then ruling for ostriches it was not surprising that the quantity of ostrich meat available for consumption was limited. Was one supposed to slice a steak off a live bird and then return it to the paddocks? Even more absurd were unconfirmed reports of ostrich farmers keeping their birds inside their houses because they were too valuable to be left out in a paddock!

Approximately five years later, ostrich advertisements in *The Weekly Times* had shrunk to one quarter of a page. A 48-month old *"proven breeding pair"* were offered for $2,000.[18] A second advertisement offered a *"Breeding Trio"* of *"proven straight birds"*. The mind boggles!

FROM FLORIDA TO SURFERS PARADISE

Florida in 1925 is worth mentioning because it offered a warm winter retreat for New Yorkers in much the same way Surfers Paradise offers a warm winter retreat to people who normally live in Sydney, Melbourne or some other southern location in Australia.

In 1925 Americans went wild about Florida, they subdivided swamps, traded in 'binders' — contracts on which only 10% had been paid and dreamed of warmth. Miami boasted 2,000 real estate offices and 25,000 agents when it had an official population of only 75,000.

The natural attractions of Queensland become very evident to the inhabitants of Melbourne in winter — particularly those who are not addicted to the seasonal insanity of 'footy'. In the early 1980s it became quite fashionable to 'have a unit in Surfers'.

This fashion together with a natural demand created a significant development boom, and in due course a (relatively mild) bubble began in Surfers Paradise apartment blocks. Surfers Paradise did not get as wild in 1981 as Florida in 1925 but it did generate some interesting stories. One of the more interesting advertisements of the era, which was fairly indicative of the speculative status of the market, appeared in the *Australian Financial Review* on 29 July 1981. It said:

"SIT BACK AND RELAX I WANT TO MAKE YOU A MILLIONAIRE.
HOW TO BREAK INTO THE SURFERS PARADISE REAL ESTATE BOOM FOR
$15,000 AND GET THE SKYROCKETING MARKET TO WORK FOR YOU!!!

Want to make 30% to 40% a year, tax free?
Yes, 30% to 40%.
Tax free!!
And without a worry in the world?
It's Real Estate. Surfers Paradise Real Estate.
The surest thing since gold was invented.
...
If you have more than $17,500 to put down, say $100,000, it doesn't take much thinking to see how indeed you could become a millionaire. Right on the beach, under the Surfers Paradise sun.
...
If you are interested telex your order to ...
And then sit back while I make you a millionaire....

COMPLETED MAY 1982. BREATHTAKING VIEWS.
BUY OFF THE PLAN FOR 10% DOWN AND MAKE MASSIVE CAPITAL GAINS. NEVER REPEATED OPPORTUNITY."

Eleven years after this advertisement appeared, Gold Coast real estate agents (not known for their pessimism) advised that the current value of units in this building was $150,000 to $220,000. The 'massive' capital gain promised in this advertisement turned out to be fairly negligible.

NEW YORK 1929, TOKYO 1989, NEW YORK (AGAIN) 1997

In the early 1700s some curious speculations evolved at around the same time involving the South Sea Company in England and the Mississippi company in France.

In both London and Paris the trading became a national spectacle in its own right. In London a large number of 'bubble' companies were formed for all sorts of crazy purposes including one which was formed:

"... for carrying on an undertaking of great advantage, but nobody to know what it is."

These two stories are described in great detail by Charles Mackay in his *Memoirs of Popular Delusions and the Madness of Crowds*. These are interesting tales which can be studied with detached amusement now that all the players are long ago dead and buried. However, the Wall Street crash of 1929 is not so unreal. Most people alive today have a relative who was alive at the time or who at the very least remembers the misery of the Great Depression which followed.

At the beginning of 1927, the Dow Jones Industrial Average stood at 155. These were prosperous times in the USA and people had plenty of money to play with. This could be geared up considerably by purchasing stocks on 'margin' of 20% or less. The Dow advanced to peak at 381 in September 1929 from which it declined to a trough of 41 in July 1932.

It is not necessary to repeat a description of the 1929 Wall Street crash because there are numerous excellent accounts of this mania readily available. Perhaps the best known author on this subject is J.K. Galbraith. His account of the Wall Street crash of 1929 discusses in great length the events leading up to the crash, its causes and aftermath.[19]

Many of the events of Wall Street repeated themselves in Australia in 1987. The pool operators who were adulated in 1929 were emulated by the Australian entrepreneurs of the mid-1980s. Credit for the purchase of shares was plentiful. Profitability was high by historic standards. A little later it will be shown how relatively speaking, the Australian stock market of 1987 almost reached the level of Wall Street in 1929.

It is also interesting to compare some of the events of 1929 with the Japanese stock market in the early 1990s. According to Galbraith, the 1929 Wall Street crash began on 29 October. A few days before there had been see-sawing prices which were beginning to cause alarm. In an attempt to settle a few nerves, a number of senior bankers and brokers met at noon on 23 October 1929 at which:

"... a decision was quickly reached to pool resources to support the market."

Galbraith describes how a *"debonair and self-confident"* Richard Whitney, at the time vice-president of the New York Stock Exchange, walked around the floor placing large orders for 15 to 20 stocks. For a day or so this worked but apart from a number of brief (and) small recoveries the market continued to decline until 1932 when it had fallen to 11% of its 1929 peak.

According to a press report in 1992, the Japanese, however, had a far more official solution even if stock market manipulation had dubious legitimacy:[20]

"Obsessed politicians, finance bureaucrats and businessmen are mulling over new schemes they hope will prop up the Japanese sharemarket next week.

"The latest plan is for securities companies to promote special 'large lot' investment trusts which supposedly would allow Japanese companies to circumvent the law which currently forbids them from buying their own shares.

"The Finance Ministry on Friday called on top executives of Nomura Securities and the firms that make up Japan's 'Big Four' securities houses, reportedly to give its unofficial blessing to the plan."

From a distance of 10,000 miles, it was a little difficult to judge the psychological state of Wall Street in early 1997. However, there was plenty of second-hand evidence to suggest that a speculative binge was in full swing. The local correspondent of *The Australian Financial Review* filed an interesting report in January 1997:[21]

> **"Sharemarket USA, *where it's all bull.***
>
> *"They crowd Internet chat rooms, gaze at the ticker.. and every day talk, talk, talk, shares, shares in these Wonder Years for America's sharemarket.*
>
> *"Women's magazines tell housewives how to start share clubs ... General magazines give share tips from TV hosts and soapie stars, ex-police chiefs, novelists and social workers.*
>
> *"TV shows on non-financial channels focus on sharemarkets past and present and or move mutual fund managers into sports star categories, and there seem to be more commercials for mutual funds than new cars.*
>
> *"Everywhere, cab-drivers, doormen and party guests talk and talk.. about shares. ...*
>
> *" 'investors' appear on TV to proudly tell how they have invested their life savings in two stocks about which they know nothing apart from their stock exchange codes and the 'fact' that they will double by August.*
>
> *"... the economy is in heaven and some gurus are forecasting a 7000 Dow by the end of March, 7600 or even 8000 by the end of 1997 and 10,000 by 2000."*

If this report was not exaggerated, many of the classical symptoms of a speculative bubble in full swing are evident even though the forecasts for the Dow in 1997 were achieved.

A more analytical assessment appeared in *Fortune* magazine in December 1996.[22] The article discussed many of the psychological symptoms such as the proliferation of investment clubs as well as economic ones such as excess liquidity in the system and market capitalisation as a proportion of Gross Domestic Product. Also discussed were the earnings and growth assumptions implicit in stock valuations at the time. Of particular interest is the market valuation compared to traditional yardsticks:[23]

> *"... **several traditional measures** – notably, price-to-book value and dividend yield – **point to a stock market that isn't just high but off the charts.**"*

Of even more interest, because it constituted criticism of established standards of value, was the fact that the author of the article then proceeded to say:

"For a variety of reasons, these measures are also of little use in gauging the market's prospects."

As we shall see, criticism of traditional yardsticks is a recognised symptom of a speculative boom.[24] But only an ostrich would have failed to notice the press reports which quoted extensively from Warren Buffett's annual newsletter to shareholders of Berkshire Hathaway Inc:[25]

"Mr Warren Buffett, the influential investment guru and billionaire has sounded a warning note about Wall Street, announcing that investors now risk paying too much for virtually all stocks in the US. ...

"Investors making purchases in overheated markets need to recognise that it may often take an extended period for the value of even an outstanding company to catch up with the price they paid."

Judging by the events which followed — the Dow Jones Industrial Average rose 20 points the following day — the comments of Buffett following similar noises from the Chairman of the Federal Reserve and the Organisation for Economic Co-operation and Development did not dent the enthusiasm of the ostriches of 1997.

THE SYMPTOMS OF A BOOM

What then are the symptoms of a boom which should enable the serious investor to exercise caution?

First and foremost a significant amount of activity operating on debt finance or 'margin' of one sort or another. In the case of futures trading only a deposit is required, similarly option purchasers achieve a great deal of leverage for a small down payment. In agriculture, leverage can be achieved by trading in animals bred for breeding other animals rather than animals bred for shearing, milking or slaughtering.

Margin trading seems to be a common feature of all speculative episodes. In the case of the Australian stock market of 1987, a great deal of this finance came from the banks. Sometimes the same thing can be achieved by making commitments prior to raising cash. This happened in the case of some property trusts in the late 1980s and when the cash could not be raised the leverage worked with a vengeance on remaining unit-holders.

A second symptom is unusual behaviour, such as office staff regularly working beyond midnight, or farmers keeping ostriches inside their houses. During the Poseidon boom, a Melbourne broker arrived at work so early and left so late that he was able to park outside his office in Collins Street every day in the one space that had been overlooked by those responsible for installing parking meters. A few years later stock exchange floor operators had so little to do that they played cricket with balls made up of rolled up paper and used rulers for bats.

A third symptom is outrageous claims by brokers and other sales agents. It is hard to believe that anyone took the claims of the agent selling apartments in Surfers Paradise seriously. But this was repeated a few years later when a Melbourne investment adviser published an advertisement which said:

> *"What's a reasonable rate of return on your money? These days I'd say 30 to 40% per annum."*

It was interesting that in February 1994, when the Australian market reached what has turned out to be a minor peak, a well known investment adviser was quoted as saying:[26]

> *"We hope that by the end of the decade the [Australian] market could reach 6000 points, although, of course, there will continue to be market fluctuations between now and then."*

But to return to the major boom of 1987, in September a securities firm published a report which contained the following forecasts:

> *"The share market now looks to have more upside than even we thought possible in the last [circular]. We believe that the [Australian] All Ordinaries Index, currently at 2160, will reach 2600 by the end of 1987 and 3500 by the end of 1988."*

While some of the quotations in this chapter originated from small organisations, this latter circular was distributed by a large and respected firm. Similar views were expressed in the press and elsewhere at around the same time. It is now a matter of record that the Australian All Ordinaries index peaked at 2312 in September 1987. It subsequently crashed to a low of 1149 the following month and traded between 1170 and 1624 in 1988.

A fourth symptom is successful speculation by non-professional operators. Quite often such people are very willing to talk about shares at social occasions and boast about their winnings. Most of the time investment professionals would find themselves talking about non-investment matters at social occasions. The sight of someone who knows little about shares holding the floor at a cocktail party talking about the stock market is a good warning sign, particularly if the audience is drinking French champagne on a fairly hum-drum occasion.

There is no surer confirmation of excessive valuations than a number of well-presented, young investment professionals saying that value-oriented investors (or some more derogatory description) do not understand this market — they are a century out of date. The phenomenon was described by Richard Band in Contrary Investing for the '90s as "widespread rejection of old standards of value"[27].

A large Japanese securities firm placed a full-page advertisement in the Australian press in 1989,[28] when the Nikkei index was 32,000, criticising the use of price/earnings ratios (see opposite).

This edited extract is a little long, but it is worth the space because of the capitalisation of the Tokyo market at the time, and because it was placed by what was then one of the largest broking houses in the world.

Notice some of the observations referred to in the preface: seductive advertising, persuasive prose and theories claimed as facts. Also the ridicule directed at dissenters is none too subtle — suggesting that groupthink may have been flourishing among Japanese brokers at the time.

Copernicus (the enlightened who had discarded old standards of value) was right for a while but Ptolemy (the unenlightened who believes in the merits of old fashioned standards such as the price/earnings ratio) was well ahead at last count. A newspaper report published after the Nikkei had subsequently fallen to 18,000, quoted an analyst as saying that:[29]

"the Tokyo market is undervalued at an adjusted price earnings ratio of about 27 times prospective consolidated profit."

COPERNICUS
or
PTOLEMY

PE-Ratios...An Outdated Criterion?
Enlighten Yourself on the Logical Market
Determinants

In this day and age, you would be considered absurd if you adhered to the Ptolemaic theory, declaring that the sun revolved around the earth. The 16th century astronomer, Copernicus, changed our way of thinking about the revolution of the universe, stating that the sun was first in existence and the earth revolved around it. The investment world conforms closely with the Copernican view of the universe. Like the sun the stock market existed first, and like the planets the investors are at its will. Some investors, critical of the Tokyo market, cling to their own theories about how investments should be evaluated, adamantly following the ancient Ptolemaic theory. They point to sky-high PE-ratios and claim that Tokyo is much too expensive and that the market is unstable ... instead of deepening their knowledge and enlightening themselves on the Copernican point of view. It is important to examine the facts.

Since Black Monday, the Tokyo market has clearly outperformed the New York and European stock markets. As the largest of the world's stock markets, Tokyo constituted 44.2% of their entire capitalisation as of December 1988. Analysis shows that Tokyo's quick rebound was a factor of market determinants which have always existed: strong earnings performance, low and stable interest rates and ample liquidity.

...

The PE-ratio, an often used measure of the relative value of a stock, merely reflects the movement of the stock market in response to these underlying market determinants.

Copernicus or Ptolemy? Enlighten yourself."

A price/earnings ratio of 27 is a considerable reduction from 80 but it was still — even at this level — somewhat questionable.

In discussing the US market at the end of 1996, an article in *Fortune* described the traditional concepts of price-to-book and dividend yield in uncomplimentary terms:[30]

> *"Furthermore, price-to-book calculations measure Machine Age capital like bricks and mortar but not the crucial stuff of the Information Age, like intellectual property ...*
>
> *As for dividend yield, stock buyback plans have become the preferred method of paying shareholders, which makes the yield nearly useless in calculating the market's value. The yield of the S&P 500 dipped below 3% – a traditional sell signal – in January 1992; since then the Dow has doubled. It now rests at a shade over 2% and is at a low for the century – in fact, and in reputation."*

While the collapse of the ostrich market of 1992 and the Japanese market of 1989 are now matters of history, perhaps we should leave it to history to pass judgement on whether Wall Street in 1997 confirms the observation that widespread rejection of old standards of value is a crucial indicator of a speculative binge in full swing.

THE LIMITS OF INVESTMENT REGULATION

Just as the Wall Street debacle of 1929 led to the establishment of the US Securities and Exchange Commission so did the Poseidon boom lead to Australian laws governing the securities industry.

Throughout the 1980s and 1990s, the volume of legislation dealing with companies and the securities industry has expanded to lengths which would have defied even the most optimistic bureaucrat ten years earlier.

The purpose of the exercise is to improve the efficiency and honesty of the system, and to protect the public. This intention is quite laudable but unfortunately, the apparent need for incessant legislative and regulatory changes suggests that the regulatory approach has yet to prove successful. It is curious that when regulatory regimes do not achieve their objective, politicians and some sections of the public place great faith in further regulation rather than repeal.

One of the most important objectives was to prevent charlatans from providing investment advice, or selling securities. To conduct either of these activities a licence is required which must be shown to a customer on demand. In practice, few customers inspect licences but licensees often include a brief statement that they are licensed on their letterhead.

The public have little knowledge of the procedures involved in obtaining a securities licence. They incorrectly assume, based on their experience of licences they understand, (e.g. driving licences) that the holder has achieved an appropriate standard of proficiency.

This is unfortunately a long way from the truth. The investment world is tolerant of a wide range of opinions and different points of view. It is not possible to assess competency to provide investment advice with the same accuracy or reliability that a physical skill such as driving a car or flying an aeroplane can be tested.

This shortcoming seems to be recognised by the Australian Law Reform Commission. In its discussion paper entitled *Collective Investment Schemes*, it was proposed that operators of these schemes should have a *"responsible entity class"* dealer's licence.[31] But yet:

> *"5.12 The Review does not consider that it is feasible to require a licensing regime for responsible entities to provide any effective measure of competence, for the same reasons that the [regulators] have not sought to use the current dealers licensing system to test for competence. The market is the only economically efficient mechanism by which the competence of a responsible entity can be judged."*

This is tacit admission that a securities licence was far more like a fishing licence than a driving licence. That is to say, if the licensee pays his registration fee, he will not get fined if he gets caught fishing. Proving that someone is not properly exercising the privileges of a securities licence has been difficult to establish.

A salesman in a smart office with a licence on display, mouthing the jargon, and making 'recommendations' is far more plausible for the existence of the licence. If there were no security licences, a member of the public would be far more cautious in dealing with 'advisers'.

As the Victorian Commissioner for Corporate Affairs said in an interview on ABC Television in 1990:

> *"A licensing system which does not work is worse than no system at all."*

As a mechanism for protecting the public, prospectus requirements and other fund-raising regulations are another aspect of corporate law which is over-rated. Indeed, as discussed below, these requirements could be having an effect directly opposite to what was intended.

We have already seen how the use of margins to achieve leverage is a symptom of a boom. One form of this is the 'dual fund' — a company with two classes of shares in roughly equal proportions. The 'income' shares receive all the income but are then redeemed at face value in 10 or 20 years time. The 'capital' shares receive no income in this period but own the company when the 'income' shares are redeemed.

On 6 August 1987, one such company — trumpeted as a unique share offer — advertised a prospectus in the *Weekend Australian*. Demand for the shares was so great that the company sought and obtained a concession from the relevant government authority to double the number of shares offered and as a result twice as many shares were issued shortly before the October 1987 crash.

The regulatory authorities will argue that it was not their fault that people subscribed for shares in this company at the top of a speculative market. If this is the case it is difficult to understand why the Australian Securities Commission is required to be involved in the first case. No matter how low-key the ASC involvement and no matter how much the ASC disclaims responsibility any involvement at all is seen by the public as a qualified stamp of approval.

In some cases prospectuses exhibit a statement that "*these shares are speculative*" on the front cover. But as we saw at the Ostrich auction in Narrandera in 1989, such semi-official warnings have no effect when groupthink is operating and may make things worse by adding to the excitement.

The authorities do not accept responsibility for the contents of a prospectus. Nevertheless prospectuses do contain a statement that they have been 'lodged' with the Australian Securities Commission. The whole exercise is time-consuming and expensive; the fees paid to lawyers and other consultants are not small. As recovery of these costs is borne by the investor, one way or another, it is sometimes difficult to see how the extensive prospectus requirements benefit the investing public.

Furthermore, the presentation of a prospectus on high quality paper, with names of prestigious firms of accountants, lawyers and other consultants, together with a statement that it has been 'lodged' with the Australian Securities Commission carries an aura of substance which is not always justified. If there were no requirements whatsoever, the average member of the public would be far more careful and would have far more chance of discriminating between quality and rubbish in commonsense ways.

The events of the 1980s demonstrated that this sort of legislation is next to useless. More crashes will bring more laws — like the introduction of the Australian Financial Institutions Commission in the wake of the collapse of Pyramid Building Society. The introduction of legislation regulating trustees of superannuation funds — partly due to the Maxwell scandal in the UK — is another example. The sight of some of the high-fliers of the 1980s in gaol may please the regulators but it is of little help to those who have lost their money — and next time around some new device will be found to make the old legislation ineffective.

In *The Great Crash 1929*, Galbraith expressed his reservations on regulation:

"... it is neither public regulation nor the improving moral tone of [the industry] which prevents these recurrent outbreaks and their aftermath.
It is the recollection of how, on some past occasion, illusion replaced reality and people got rimmed ...

By the sixties this memory had dimmed. Almost everything described in this book had reappeared, sometimes in only a slightly different guise."

There are three messages in this foray into the question of regulation.

First, the laws currently being passed to protect the investor will probably not work in the next boom.

Second, the licensing system in the securities industry creates an illusion of government supervision; of competence and integrity which is not always justified. In any event theft, broadly interpreted, cannot be prevented. History has demonstrated many ways of disenfranchising clients, shareholders, creditors and investors which may be judged improper but are not illegal.

Investors who rely on the regulation of the Corporations Law for their protection may subsequently enjoy the sight of convicted rogues being temporarily deprived of their liberty, but this does not solve the problems of the family budget. The following exchange took place at a public hearing of a parliamentary committee:[32]

*"**ASC Chairman**: ... One financial adviser has just been gaoled for four years in Western Australia for taking just under a million dollars worth of client money ..."*

*"**Committee Chair**: ... You say someone has been gaoled. Therefore, maybe the law has not provided the safeguards anyway.*

*"**ASC Chairman**: It is certainly not a guarantee."*

The third message of the history of regulation relates to the operation of organisations such as banks, building societies and life insurance companies. These organisations have traditionally earned a somewhat conservative reputation.

However, a significant factor in the Savings and Loans disaster, mirrored to some extent in Australian institutions, was implicit official support. In the case of the US 'thrift' it was deposit insurance; in the case of Pyramid Building Society is was the gazetting of 'trustee investment status'.

The combination of an illusion of safety for depositors — partially caused by official patronage — and a speculative mortgage book proved disastrous in the end.

These examples seem to suggest that there is no half-way house. If regulation is intended to make such institutions safe, then it had better do so. If regulation merely creates an illusion of safety, then it will be exploited and gullible members of the public will suffer.

There may be some preventative benefit in prosecution but it proved largely ineffective in discouraging excesses in the 1980s. In 1992, Henry Bosch, former head of the National Companies and Securities Commission wrote:[33]

"Rich and clever crooks will always exploit the system. The demands of evidentiary and procedural requirements also mean that few criminal charges ever will be laid. Most corporate malefactors, therefore will remain untouched by our criminal law."

Since this article was written, the Australian Securities Commission has shown commendable determination in pursuit of a number of high profile malefactors of the 1980s. Except for one case where a fugitive has managed to prevent extradition to Australia on the grounds of ill-health, the Commission had some remarkable successes which may improve the preventative value of the law.

There seems little doubt that prevention is far superior to conviction after the event, which is one of the reasons for licensing. In this respect, publicity may be a more effective weapon than licensing, as the UK satirical magazine *Private Eye* has demonstrated in London.

There may be some merit in providing qualified immunity from defamation and/or libel actions when the subject is the business operation of an investment adviser, dealer or prospectus. Even without such qualified immunity experienced journalists have been able to ridicule defective prospectuses. For example, late in 1996, "Pierpont" of *The Australian Financial Review* reported that:[34]

> "The search for Trust of the Year has flagged a little in recent months for lack of entries. This week, however, a Melbourne reader has provided a worthy contender by sending Pierpont the prospectus for ...
>
> "... a particularly free trust, untrammelled by pettifogging red tape and giving generous discretion to its managers.
>
> "... Let's hope the float is highly successful, because if only a few punters subscribe the value of their investment is going to be heavily eroded by the prospectus expenses."

It is unlikely that many prospective subscribers read Pierpont's article, or for that matter the prospectus. The main virtue of such comment lies in the adverse publicity for firms and organisations named in the prospectus and/or press report whose reputation would be dented if the report is accurate. Tarnished reputations in the securities industry are a significant obstacle to the attraction of business.

The excessive regulation of capital raising has also had some serious consequences for genuine entrepreneurs which are quite perverse. For an organisation the size of one of the major banks, the legal fees and other expenses in issuing a prospectus do not constitute a large percentage of the capital raised. But in the case of someone with a bright idea (scientific or otherwise) seeking to raise some risk capital, such expenses are very high.

In consequence, many scientific developments may have been lost to the country. This is not because risk capital is not available — as the ostrich has demonstrated. Contrary to the efficient market theory, many people are happy to back speculative ventures; in many cases the more exciting and riskier the better.

A second perverse effect of this regulation was its part in stimulating demand for graduates in accounting and law. One wonders if this has not contributed to the fact that these undergraduate disciplines may be attracting more than their fair share of the most able young people in the country at the expense of non-medical sciences. This is evident in the table below which shows the Tertiary Entrance Rank requirements for 'first round' offers of places at Melbourne University in 1997:

COURSE	TERTIARY ENTRANCE RANK
Law	98.75
Commerce	88.15
Engineering	76.40
Science	76.05

WHAT, THEN, ARE THE LESSONS OF HISTORY?

Despite the advances in science and technology, human emotions still work much as they did a millennium ago. As we have seen, most of the excesses of markets have been emotionally-based. While history may not repeat itself, and it would be highly unlikely to do so exactly, it would be wise to assume that another boom and bust will happen somewhere, some day.

For the purposes of making investment decisions, the historical record would suggest that:

(a) Speculative booms and busts in particular stocks or market sectors are likely to recur. People thought that the Wall Street speculation of 1929 would not recur. But it did recur in 1989 in Tokyo, and with a vengeance. The jury is yet to consider its verdict on US market levels of 1997, despite the financial turmoil in Asia.

(b) When a boom does occur, the financial community will tend to reinforce rather than question the absurdity of valuations at the time.

(c) When the bust happens there will be an avalanche of legislation to follow which will not prevent previous excesses reappearing in some new guise.

(d) The history of the last boom, and a forthright recognition of the propensity of men and women to behave like sheep is a far better defence against the next boom and bust than legislation.

(e) Investors who rely on government regulation as protection from incompetence and malpractice are exposing themselves to considerable risks.

Richard Band summarised this lesson succinctly:[35]

"Three hundred years of booms and busts demonstrate that human nature changes little, if at all, over the centuries. During a credit-induced economic boom, this illusion takes on a sheen of plausibility. The inescapable lesson of history, however, is that wealth building takes time, work, good saving habits and – perhaps most important – the emotional discipline to steer away from investment fads."

This brief summary of some of the important bubbles and busts of the last 30 years should question the rationality among capital market participants – one of the most important assumptions of the 'efficient market' theory.

Were these booms, busts and other aberrations the work of 'efficient markets' or were they the result of varying degrees of temporary insanity and/or groupthink among investors, trustees, and others operating in the financial services industry? In the preface to the 1852 edition of his *Memoirs of Extraordinary Delusions and the Madness of Crowds*, Charles Mackay wrote:

"In reading the history of nations, we find that, like individuals, they have their whims and their peculiarities; their seasons of excitement and recklessness, when they care not what they do. We find that whole communities suddenly fix their minds upon one object, and go mad in its pursuit; that millions of people become simultaneously impressed with one delusion, and run after it, till their attention is caught by some new folly more captivating than the first."

Perhaps the most important lesson of history is that investors who fail to study history itself are ill-equipped for their task.

There may be an argument for the inclusion of a chronicle of stock market crashes and investment scams in the compulsory curriculum for secondary schools. This may not be as interesting as the paper-gambling involved in 'share games', but if self-funded retirement is to become the 'norm' of the future, elementary teaching of this sort of history may pay handsome public dividends in the decades ahead.

Chapter 3

General Features of Different Asset Classes

PROPERTY, BUSINESSES AND DEBT — THE BASIC BUILDING BLOCKS

DESPITE THE establishment of stock markets, options markets and a variety of other sophisticated developments of the last century or so there are still only three basic sorts of investment or primary 'asset classes' — property, businesses and debt.

For many people the family home is a substantial proportion of their net worth — often more than 100%. But given the requirement — discussed in the next chapter — for investments to generate a reasonable return, does the family home constitute an investment? There is perhaps some validity in the argument that owner occupiers would otherwise need to pay rent and this creates an implicit income in home-ownership.

However, once 'lifestyle' type assets go beyond satisfying the *need* for somewhere to live, they tend to be income-consuming rather than income-producing. While people need some*where* to live they also need something to live *on*. In the discussion which follows property is taken to mean 'investment property' as distinct from owner-occupied residential property, hobby farms and recreational retreats.

Until quite recently investment in commercial property was beyond the reach of people of modest means and large private investors were still restricted to flats, small commercial buildings and private syndicates.

The advent of the listed trust has brought investment in large office blocks, shopping centres, factories and warehouses within the means of most investors. From a tiny beginning in 1969, with a prospectus for just $500,000, the total capitalisation of listed trusts had reached $10 billion in 1992, and roughly $20 billion in 1997.[1]

This moderately-sized market provides the private investor — and small superannuation fund — with reasonable choice and an alternative to residential property and small commercial buildings. However, the large superannuation fund may still wish to hold its property investments directly. The question as to whether property investments should be held directly or through some pooled arrangement is discussed later.

The next major class of investments is ordinary shares, sometimes called equities in Australia and usually called 'common stocks' in the USA. Ordinary shares are really a form of listed businesses which owe their origin to the development of the public company. This came into existence when partners in a business were allowed to incorporate and enjoy limited liability — the most they could lose was the amount of capital they had subscribed plus any outstanding amount on partly-paid shares.

Prior to the creation of the limited liability concept, proprietors would be reluctant to relinquish control, however the legalisation of limited liability of shareholders broke the nexus between ownership and control; businesses were then able to expand well beyond the means of normal individual proprietors.

Not all business proprietors enjoy limited liability which can have severe consequences if things go wrong; the problems recently endured by the 'Names' of the London Lloyds insurance operation provide an example. It would be difficult to think of a company listed in Australia which does not have limited shareholder liability, and it is relatively simple to check for Ltd or Limited at the end of a company's name.

Investment in shares or equities is what most people normally associate with stock exchange trading. The essential feature is that ownership of equities or ordinary shares in a limited company represents a pro-rata ownership, but not operational control, of a business. Shareholders elect directors, participate in profits by way of dividends and are entitled to attend, speak and vote at company meetings.

The third major asset class is fixed-interest securities or debt. Investors who do not wish to invest in property or businesses can lend their money to some other party including governments, banks, companies and private individuals. This type of investment can come in a variety of forms.

Funds on deposit with a bank or other organisation are usually available at short notice with variable interest rates; alternatively these deposits can be fixed for varying terms. Fixed-interest securities issued by governments or large companies can be obtained by subscription to a prospectus or purchased through the secondary market; money can be lent out on mortgage.

The essential feature of a fixed-interest investment is that the investment has a known face value payable on maturity, or in some other agreed manner, and interest is paid on the outstanding principal at a rate that is either fixed or varied in some other predetermined way.

In addition to property, shares and debt, there are indexed securities, hybrids such as convertible notes, redeemable preference shares and 'synthetic instruments' or 'derivatives' such as futures, options contracts and warrants.

DERIVATIVES — THE TULIPS OF THE 1990s?

There always seems to be a new supply of individuals who believe that they have discovered the ultimate secret to the 'fast buck' in the stock market. Until experience teaches them otherwise, the incredible leverage available in options, futures and warrants will continue to attract the optimistic speculator and the derivatives junkie. US author David Dreman, discussed at some length the poor record of stock speculators. He then commented:[2]

"Large numbers of investors use options as a massive crap shoot in an all-or-nothing manner. From the previous indications of market timing and stock selection, most often it is nothing."

Conservative investors think options, futures and warrants are too speculative to be considered by any rational investor. For those who do not understand them, this may be so. But it would be interesting to discover how many investors who feel this way are quite happy to belong to a superannuation fund which deals in derivatives, buy units in a managed fund which uses derivatives or deposit money with a bank which has substantial positions in bond futures.

For this reason, it is not possible to ignore derivatives just by avoiding them directly. There is however, a more important reason why thoughtful investor-citizens should acquaint themselves with derivatives. If these markets are allowed to expand their trading activities indefinitely, there is a point at which, in adverse conditions, they could threaten the financial system including the banks.

The reason for this threat lies in the cash movement disciplines or margin calls required by derivative clearing systems. When shares issued by public companies rise or fall no cash changes hands. Consequently an adverse change in market prices will not create any cash pressure except on margin traders and paper losers who have used their shares for security.

Cash option buyers and scrip-covered option writers are not subject to margin calls, but in most other cases the clearing of exchange-traded derivative contracts creates an immediate daily requirement for losers to make good their unrealised losses in cash — the margin call.[3]

In some cases the losses can be so large that speculators are unable to cover them. In futures markets, defaulters are closed out forthwith, thereby creating additional pressure. An example of this occurred in January 1980 when the price of one ounce of gold fell by $US 200 overnight and Sydney futures contracts, which had been trading at a premium to the gold price, fell to a substantial discount to absorb the forced selling. As a result the price of futures contracts fell considerably more than the underlying commodity.

If participants in the market are unable to cover their position then their Clearing Member will be required to make up the loss. If a Clearing Member is unable to cover the position then it will be declared a defaulter and the Clearing House is left to clean up the mess **between** other Clearing Members. If the Clearing House then fails, other Clearing Members will be left holding contracts some of which will be in default from the Clearing House but they will still be liable to their clients on the other side of the contract.[4]

A casual observer of the trading floor at the Sydney Futures Exchange may get the impression of an unusually energetic crowd at a teams' tiddlywinks contest. However, the business is deadly serious despite the colourful uniforms and eccentric gesticulations, as demonstrated in the table of selected statistics opposite:

Sydney Futures Exchange — Turnover 1996

	TURNOVER VOLUME (million of contracts)	CONTRACT VALUE ($)	TURNOVER BY VALUE ($bn)
Share Price Index	2.7	55,000	150
3-year bonds	9.2	100,000	920
10-year bonds	5.3	100,000	530

Thus, in Share Price Index contracts alone, the daily trading volume is typically 10,000 contracts with a face value of the order of $500 million. The annual turnover by contract value is thus $150 billion or 25% of Australian Gross Domestic Product. However, Share Price Index contracts are relatively unimportant compared to the turnover in three and ten year bond contracts. A summary booklet prepared by the Australian Financial Markets Association reported that the notional value of all contracts traded on the Sydney Futures Exchange in the 1996/97 financial year was $8,711 billion which is approximately $500,000 per Australian citizen.

Does this level of activity allow investors with a genuine interest in hedging their positions or managing financial risks to do so? Or is the sheer magnitude of the turnover evidence of speculation as the dominant motive of traders? Does this not create a new kind of risk, concentrated in Clearing Houses and Clearing Members (including some banks) which, if it grew big enough, could threaten the whole financial system in the event of unusually large movements in stock markets or interest rates?

This is not the place to attempt an answer to this question. But by asking it, investors may question the economic value of exchange-traded derivative markets and trustees of superannuation funds may wonder if their desire for performance is not contributing towards the creation of a monster which, one day, may lead to a repeat of the US experience in 1929 — and create the environment for a repeat of its aftermath.

According to J.K. Galbraith, trading on margin was a significant contributor to the excesses of 1929 and the misery which followed.[5] It might be worth mentioning that margins at the time were around 10% — by comparison, the initial margin on the Australian Share Price Index contract in late 1997 was approximately 7%.

The strategy suggested by this discussion is that ordinary investors should either avoid derivative contracts or use them sparingly, exercise extreme care if operating on margin and properly investigate the derivative activities of any collective investments (including superannuation funds) in which they are involved.

Those who have reservations about the threat which derivatives pose should ask questions when suitable opportunities arise and not be satisfied by glib answers about managing risk. What about the new form of 'melt-down' risk created in the clearing system? Perhaps the financial system as a whole is no longer as secure as it would be if financial derivatives had not been invented.

RISK, LIQUIDITY AND VOLATILITY

Readers will recall from earlier (page 9) how investment theorists have confused volatility and risk. The continued use of the word risk to describe volatility has made it difficult to use the word risk unambiguously. It has also become fashionable to describe the lack of ready saleability as liquidity risk. As a result the three concepts of risk, volatility and liquidity have become confused.

It is difficult to find another word for risk, but why should it be necessary to do so if people who should know better are too lazy to spell or pronounce volatility and misuse risk instead. Accordingly 'risk' is used here with its normal meaning — 'chance of bad consequence'.[6]

In any event risk does not manifest itself in adverse share price fluctuations for genuine long-term investors unless:

(a) There has been a deterioration in the company's long-term prospects

(b) The price at which shares were purchased exceeded the intrinsic value of the business

(c) The funds invested in shares were needed for a short-term purpose such as a holiday or a new car, and the money should not have been used to buy shares anyway.

This last example — investing savings for a holiday in the stock market — illustrates the point that risk cannot be considered in isolation from the purpose or circumstances of the investor. Risk — like beauty — is in the eyes of the beholder. We will return to this topic in the next chapter.

Liquidity is used to describe the ease and speed with which an investment can be bought and/or sold. Bank accounts are highly liquid. Government bonds, in reasonable parcels, are fairly liquid. Listed property trust units are fairly liquid while most of the underlying property is not.

In the unlisted property trust debacle of the early 1990s, trust operators were required to undertake to repurchase investors' units subject to certain conditions. Unfortunately most of the trust assets could not be sold quickly when unit-holders decided *en masse* that they wished to redeem their investment. Although the catalyst for this avalanche of redemption requests was probably doubts about the underlying property valuations, those involved learnt an important lesson — lack of liquidity can cause business risks to an organisation subject to liquidity demands on the other side. However, lack of liquidity, *per se*, is not necessarily a risk for a long-term investor.

The following examples are intended to illustrate the differences between risk, volatility and liquidity from the perspective of a genuinely long-term investor.

Mortgages – a safe, illiquid and non-volatile investment

When investors lend their money on first mortgage against a conservatively valued property, with a sound tenant, and with a reasonable margin between the rent and interest as well as a margin between the property value and the principal of the mortgage, they may not be taking any significant risk. However, the investor must wait until the date the principal is due — which may be progressively over the term of the contract — for repayment or return of principal.

Although developments are taking place which could improve the liquidity of mortgages, there is no ready market in mortgages at the present time and consequently they are fairly illiquid.

Government bonds – a safe, fairly liquid and volatile investment

Commonwealth government bonds, assuming the question of default can be ignored, carry no risk that an interest or capital payment will not be met.

In sufficient quantities (e.g. $10 million) these securities are actively traded and consequently they are very liquid. In recent years smaller investors have become more involved and the liquidity of smaller parcels of, say, $50,000 has improved. A private investor may need to accept a small discount to sell such a parcel quickly.

On the other hand government securities fluctuate in price as a result of changes in interest rates. When interest rates are 15% per annum a security with a 'coupon' of 7% and 20 years to maturity would trade at a deep discount on its face value. Conversely a 20-year stock with a 15% coupon would trade at a significant premium on its face value when interest rates are 7%.

Bond traders talk about the 'duration' or weighted effective term to maturity of government bonds. The longer the duration, the higher the volatility. Short duration bonds, however, are not particularly volatile. For example, a 1% change in interest rates will produce a 1% change in price for a bond with a duration of 12 months. Government bonds are thus (with some qualification) riskless, reasonably liquid and, except for short-dated issues, volatile.

Property – a moderately safe and non-volatile but illiquid investment

The safety of property as an investment depends on numerous factors including the terms of existing tenancies, the financial standing of tenants and the likely terms of new or renewal tenancies when existing leases expire or tenants leave. Because rent is part of the normal operating cost of businesses it generally ranks ahead of proprietors' interests which makes property-ownership less risky than owning a business with the same turnover. However, there is always the risk of tenant bankruptcy, excessive construction leading to an oversupply of vacant space in the same area and new buildings attracting tenants on more generous terms.

Except in severe recessions and wild booms property prices tend to be fairly stable. Property is less volatile than shares although some of this is spurious because properties are valued less frequently than shares.

While both the risk and volatility of investment property tends to be below that of shares, most investment properties are illiquid. It is not possible to sell a $100 million property as quickly as $100 million in government bonds or ordinary shares.

Property is therefore fairly illiquid, reasonably stable in normal circumstances and modestly risky.

Shares are volatile but liquidity and safety are variable

It seems well accepted that shares are volatile, and as far as major companies are concerned liquidity should not be a problem for private investors. For very large institutions liquidity may be a problem except in a handful of stocks. However, in secondary stocks, liquidity can (at times) be a problem for private investors.

The question of risk (as distinct from volatility) is not a simple consideration. Risk depends on a number of factors such as quality of management, economic conditions, the nature of the business, balance sheet structure and perhaps, most importantly, the relationship between the share price and the intrinsic value of the enterprise. The share price of the most conservatively-financed organisation, operating in a stable industry with excellent management, can often reach levels at which the purchase of its shares is extremely risky.

It is not correct to say that shares in food-processing companies are always less risky than shares in mining companies. The food processing industry may be far more stable than mining, but there may be times when share prices of companies in the food industry may be so high relative to the prices of mining companies that mining shares may be less risky than shares of companies operating in the food-processing industry.

Finally, we must consider the extra dimensions involved in owning foreign assets. Much the same considerations apply except for the additional dimension of foreign exchange 'risk'. The attitude of most investors worldwide, for which accounting 'standards' are partly to blame, is that any investment denominated in some foreign currency is more risky than a comparable investment in local currency.

If an investor is subject to known obligations fixed in local currency (in this case Australian dollars) then exposure to currency fluctuations may indeed constitute risk. But if an investor has no specific fixed obligation and is investing for the long term, then greater diversification, and therefore a reduction in risk, may be achieved by investing offshore — other things being equal.

Using the local currency as a frame of reference to assess risk can be narrow-minded. If long-term investors have 25% of their assets in foreign securities which exchange risk should they be worried about? The 25% offshore or the 75% left behind? Generally speaking foreign assets have greater volatility when measured in local currency but the overall risk of an equity portfolio which includes foreign equities could well be lower than one which does not.

CASH AND FIXED-INTEREST INVESTMENTS

Investment in debt, or fixed-interest securities, comes in two varieties. First, there are assets such as bank deposits at call, where the value of the principal is not subject to price fluctuations but where rate of interest is subject to market forces. Secondly, the rate of interest payable on the principal is fixed until maturity but investors who sell prior to maturity are subject to price fluctuations which may be favourable or unfavourable.

In this respect, many investors expect the return on their investments to increase if interest rates rise. Some people are therefore surprised to learn that when interest rates rise the price of a 10-year government bond will decline, and consequently the return to investors will have fallen if they measure their returns by market values, even though the full return of principal at maturity is not in doubt. Conversely, when interest rates fall the market prices of fixed-interest securities will rise. The extent of any price fluctuation depends on the change in interest rate and the 'effective term' of the security. Generally speaking, the longer the period to maturity the greater the sensitivity to fluctuations in interest rates.

Sometimes it is possible to invest in securities which give the investor a redemption option. If interest rates rise, investors can redeem their original investment and reinvest at higher interest rates, while if interest rates fall the market price of their asset will have risen. An example of this security was Australian Savings Bonds issued in the early 1980s, although rationing prevented a really active market from developing.

Security is an important aspect of any 'cash' or fixed-interest investment. The history of events such as Pyramid Building Society, Associated Securities Limited, Estate Mortgage Trust and Rothwells Limited suggests most non-professional investors might be well advised to concentrate on security and accept the going interest rate. Investors who need the extra one or two per cent are often unable to wear the risk.

Assuming they have satisfied themselves as to the safety of the banking system as a whole, most investors should probably restrict their fixed-interest investments to bank deposits, short-term government and bank-guaranteed securities, and packaged products restricted to these assets. Such packaged products would include cash management trusts, trustee company money market funds, and life office and friendly society bonds. In purchasing 'packaged' products the quality of the packaging (i.e. the strength of the underwriting institution) will require some analysis.

Banks and other financial institutions may not require as much attention as less familiar organisations but investors who place funds on deposit without satisfying themselves as to the safety of what they are doing are in much the same position as purchasers of second-hand cars who do not insist on a mechanic's inspection. As far as the banks are concerned, one wonders, for example, how many people have bothered to find out exactly what the Reserve Bank does (and does not) guarantee.

Building societies and finance companies have been omitted from this list because they are not supervised by the Reserve Bank and because they have caused depositing investors many problems in the last 20 years. On the other hand they often offer depositors a higher standard of service, and if this is important to the investor more detailed investigation may be justified. But the credit assessment involves more than ascertaining parentage, board composition or the existence of government regulation, patronage or support. It should not be forgotten that Pyramid Building Society enjoyed authorised trustee status — as gazetted by the Victorian government — at the time of its collapse.

If, as is often the case, the purpose of fixed-interest investment is to hold funds in a form which makes them readily available for personal emergencies or alternative investment opportunities, they need to be available at short notice and should be as secure as possible.

Unless the additional margin available on riskier fixed-interest investment is substantially higher in the future than it has been in the past, the rate of interest on fixed-interest securities will remain a secondary consideration in most cases. Unfortunately, offering high interest rates is often a sign of impending trouble, as was demonstrated in the debacle of Pyramid Building Society. Investors who are not in the business of lending money or trading fixed-interest securities should perhaps leave the risks of adventurous fixed-interest investment to someone else unless they have the skills to conduct a proper credit assessment.

INVESTMENT PROPERTY

It may be a little frivolous to refer to shops, offices, warehouses and factories as income-producing investment property while describing residential, recreational and agricultural real estate as income-consuming. But, is there not an element of truth in this comment if investors are honest with themselves when they do their sums?

For example, many people reflecting on their previous home when they move, think that they have done exceedingly well out of residential property. They remember the original purchase price and the eventual sale, but they usually forget the transaction costs, rates, maintenance, redecoration, renovation and improvements.

This is not to suggest that people who buy houses to live in are stupid — far from it. Home ownership carries an implicit (and tax free) income as a result of saving rental which would otherwise need to be paid from after-tax income, and there are other important non-financial aspects of home ownership. But the purchase of residential property for investment purposes is an entirely different proposition.

The gross rental income from residential property is usually around 6% of the capital value, out of which the owner has to pay rates and maintenance, leaving approximately 4% per annum after these expenses. The returns may be somewhat better where the property is specifically built and located for rental. Unlike owner occupation, where the implicit rental is tax free, the net income from an investment property is taxable.

Besides this low-income return, residential tenants tend to have more votes than landlords and, in most parts of the world, the law tends to be biased in favour of tenants as far as financial delinquency and liability for damage is concerned which may also affect the net return. There have also been times when governments have bestowed the advantages of fixed rentals on incumbent tenants while they proceeded to debase their currency. Many tenants in London today still enjoy residential rentals set at 1970 levels; in the meantime, residential properties subject to these rent controls have caused substantial losses to the original landlords if they needed to sell.

In common with residential property, rural land provides a low income in relation to its capital value. When investment involves the operation of a farm as well, the investor is buying into an agricultural business which will not disappoint those seeking difficulty and challenge. People with years and sometimes generations of experience and whose fortitude has been toughened by drought, bushfires and other hardships do not often make a profit which compensates them for the time and effort they expend working their farms.

Consequently if they allowed themselves (and their family-helpers) a reasonable wage in their calculations, the profitability of most farms would be very small except in unusually good years. It may be possible to purchase farms in difficult times and sell in booms, but this sort of trading is very different from purchasing agricultural property as an investment.

Despite these difficulties a number of professional people seem to seek agricultural land with a religious fervour as an 'investment'. Many years ago when the top marginal tax rate was over 60%, when clearing trees, installing dams[7] and other capital improvements were encouraged through the tax system, these tax benefits may have enabled a reasonable return to be achieved, but this no longer applies. The desire to own land is quite a natural human emotion, but investment decisions should be based on logic and analysis rather than emotion.

A difficult aspect of property investment is the achievement of adequate diversification. A prospective landlord may look at the list of tenants in a building and reflect that they are all of the highest calibre and on long leases. If the general market in the area is declining, then it will be difficult to keep the tenants on expiry because they will be keenly sought by other landlords, and in the meantime any rental reviews will be problematical. For this reason having a diversified list of tenants within the same building is not sufficient diversification. What is really required is a spread of property by geographical location as well as type.

It will therefore require an investment fund of some magnitude to achieve adequate diversification if property investments are directly held. Except for such large institutions and pension funds, indirect property investment will be inevitable if reasonable diversification is to be achieved.

A frequent cause of inadequate diversification with direct investment is parochialism. Small investors resident in Melbourne for example would naturally tend to select their first investment properties locally. As the problems of the early 1990s demonstrated, this habit may concentrate assets in a local area subject to widespread difficulties. Investments spread interstate is a significant improvement. If practicable, an international spread would be better still.

The average investor and moderately-sized superannuation fund is therefore restricted to some form of property pool to avoid the risks associated with inadequate diversification while acquiring a beneficial interest in major city buildings, shopping centres and so on, both locally and internationally.

ORDINARY SHARES

The purchase of ordinary shares listed on a stock exchange generally confers on the purchaser a pro-rata beneficial interest in the business. Shares in most of the more important companies can be readily bought or sold. Share prices are quite volatile, particularly in the case of mining or exploration companies. However, this volatility should not be confused with risk.

Share prices fluctuate but the long-term value of the underlying business tends to wobble. Very few major companies disappear without trace but they do, however, suffer their ups and downs, their good years and bad years, and periodic write-downs when segments of the business trade poorly. Thus, risk in relation to shares must be based on both an analysis of the nature of the undertaking and its financial statements as well as an assessment of a fair price for the shares. There is no such thing as a risk-free business, but much of the risk involved in share investment is the direct result of paying excessive prices for the shares.

Conducting such an analysis may sound daunting but it is essential if speculation is to be avoided. To some extent the job can be made appreciatively easier, and the risks associated with selecting individual securities can be removed, by purchasing shares in conservatively-operated listed investment companies, listed equity trusts or unlisted equity trusts. If the underlying portfolios are fairly 'typical' then the investor should enjoy fairly 'typical' results. This indirect approach nevertheless removes the possibility of benefits derived from superior selection of individual securities — but an investor who does not make the effort can hardly expect this benefit for nothing.

While equity 'pools' can be used to achieve 'normal' results and avoid the risks associated with individual stocks, this approach will not help investors avoid the risk associated with the stock market as a whole being priced at speculative levels. Consequently, any direct or indirect purchase of ordinary shares requires, as a minimum, periodic assessment of overall market levels.

There may be isolated exceptions to this requirement but they would be extremely rare. Contrary to the 'efficient' market theory, it is possible for individual securities to be underpriced when the market as a whole is overpriced but special care is required in these circumstances.

LONG–TERM RETURNS

In formulating a long-term investment policy, a useful starting point is an assessment of the likely long-term returns to be achieved from a 'typical' and conservatively-selected portfolio chosen from the three basic asset classes of property, equities and debt. Ideally this assessment will need to take into account any taxes on income and capital profits as well as inflation.

Inflation is a particularly important consideration in the long term — bearing in mind the fact that the Australian currency will have lost at least 98% of its purchasing power in the 20th century.

In the case of cash investments it might be argued that there is no protection from inflation, however there is some logic (and supporting historical data) in the suggestion that interest rates will tend to be higher in periods of high inflation and lower in periods of low inflation. Unfortunately there is no simple formula such as *"cash interest rates are equal to the rate of inflation plus five per cent per annum"*, and the taxation system heavily discriminates against fixed-interest investors.

Let us say, for the sake of argument, that the formula given above holds. Then with inflation at 10%, interest rates will be 15% and with inflation at zero the rate of interest will be 5%. An investor of modest means subject to a marginal rate of tax of (say) 30% will receive 10.5% after tax when the rate of inflation is 10% and 3.5% when the rate of inflation is zero. The investor's real net rate of return — the rate of interest net of tax and inflation — is thus 0.5% when inflation is 10% and 3.5% when inflation is zero. (This example illustrates how fixed-interest investors tend to be better off in a low interest rates/low inflation environment compared to a high interest rates/high inflation environment — but one wonders how many people were able to see it that way.)

In the case of longer-dated fixed-interest securities, the effect of rising inflation (if it also leads to a rise in interest rates) can be quite devastating because the rise in interest rates will cause a decline in the market value of the security while the real value of what remains is being simultaneously reduced by the effect of inflation.

It might be reasonable to suggest that the gross rate of return on cash investments may exceed the rate of inflation by a small margin, but the net real rate of return for most investors will be either negligible or negative. The likely return from long-dated fixed-interest securities is a complex mathematical issue involving 'yield curves', 'duration' and 'reinvestment rates'. In the long run the various fluctuations should offset one another and the return from longer-dated securities should be similar to the return from cash investments.

It is often argued that the yield on fixed-interest securities normally increases with the term to maturity and, in consequence, the return from holding long-dated securities will exceed the return from short-dated securities over a length of time, sufficient for the fluctuations to even out. However, there have also been extended periods when the 'yield curve' has been inverse — the yield on longer securities has been less than the yield of shorter-dated stock.

It is not surprising that in periods of high inflation investors turn to shares and property to protect the real value of their investments. The long-term relationship between share prices and inflation is a matter of some dispute, so perhaps we should deal with property first.

Real property consists of land and buildings. Unlike the supply of paper money, the supply of land is fixed for practical purposes. (The geological observation that in 10 million years' time San Francisco will be a suburb of Los Angeles is beyond the investment concept of long term!) As the supply is fixed it would be reasonable to expect that 'broadly speaking' land values will move in line with Gross Domestic Product, or at the very least the rate of inflation as measured by a general index such as the GDP implicit price deflator. (Maybe agricultural land is a better investment than cash after all!)

The cost of buildings depends on the cost of labour and materials which (bearing in mind the 98% decline in the value of money this century) are relatively stable in real terms. Unfortunately, rents and the market value of established buildings are subject to the laws of supply and demand even though their replacement cost may be inflation-proof.

Existing buildings deteriorate with age and consequently the supply of accommodation will decline in the absence of new construction. Even if there is no growth in demand, the deterioration of existing buildings will eventually lead to absorption of vacant space and then demand will increase rents to the point at which developers find it attractive to construct new buildings. Growth in demand will accelerate the process.

In consequence the market value of new buildings will tend to fluctuate about an equilibrium based on the cost of replacing their economic value. Similarly, rents on new accommodation will fluctuate about a level at which developers will find new construction attractive. Rents on older buildings would normally be at a discount to the rent levels of new buildings.

Thus the effect of supply and demand will tend to maintain the real value of commercial properties and rents. This general rule is subject to the proviso that buildings deteriorate with age and the existence of cyclical fluctuations in rents and property values. In the case of listed trusts there will be some additional fluctuation of unit prices about underlying values.

Extended data on property prices is difficult to obtain. Buildings worth around $250 million change hands infrequently, whereas it would be unusual for some of the shares of a listed company capitalised at $250 million not to trade every business day.

In the UK, a property consultant suggested that lack of quantitative data was one cause of the relative unpopularity of property among UK pension funds.[8] In the process, the consultant provided an estimate of an index of property prices over the period 1971-1993. This period was highly inflationary, as recorded by the experience of the (appropriately named) UK Retail Prices Index which rose by a factor of 7 over the same period.

The graph below shows an index on UK property, relative to the Retail Prices Index, over this period. This is consistent with the argument of long-term maintenance of real value subject to some large cyclical fluctuations and deterioration with age.

The Real Price of UK Property 1971–1993 (1980 = 100)

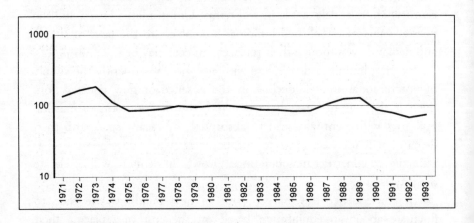

With listed property trusts, there is an additional feature of prices fluctuating about underlying property values. However, price and accumulation indices for listed Australian property trusts have now been published since December 1979. The graph below shows the Australian Stock Exchange Property Trust Price Index, relative to the Consumer Price Index, since 1979.

The Real ASX Property Trust Price Index 1979–1997

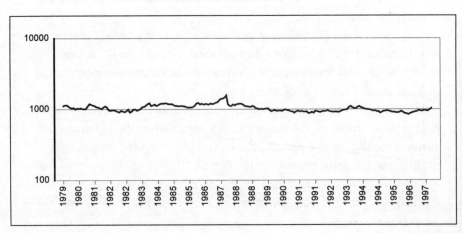

Once again, this graph is consistent with broad maintenance of real value, subject to cyclical fluctuation. If the reader accepts the argument that property prices will, with qualification, retain their real level over a long period of time, irrespective of the rate of inflation, then an estimate of the income is also required.

Roughly speaking the point at which rentals generate new office development seems to be 8% of capital value. Thus the initial gross yield on a new commercial building will be around 8% per annum. As the land content of commercial buildings is typically 30%, the balance (70%) needs to be written off over the economic life of the building. This adjustment is necessary for the purposes of this calculation irrespective of whether there is an accounting obligation to do so.

Taking a typical economic life of (say) 35 years the adjustment for deterioration of the building component is 70/35 or 2% per annum. The real return after allowing for building deterioration will be approximately 8% less 2% or 6% per annum.

This estimate can be further substantiated by comparing the Australian Stock Exchange Price and Accumulation indices. Unfortunately it is not possible to make a direct comparison on a year-by-year basis because listed trusts sometimes vary their distribution dates and frequency of payment. However, if we divide the Accumulation Index by the corresponding price index at monthly intervals and plot the result then the slope of the graph (on a semi-logarithmic scale) will provide an average estimate of the income component of total return. This is shown in the graph below. The slope of the graph is roughly 8% per annum.

ASX Property Trust Accumulation Index divided by Price Index, 1979–1997

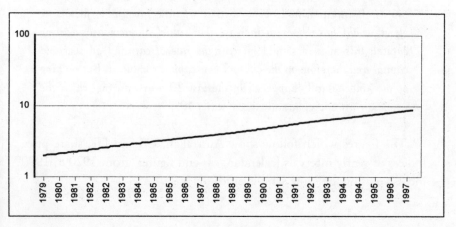

SHARE PRICES AND INFLATION

Property investors achieve their returns from rent and price fluctuations which in the long term should be roughly equal to the rate of inflation less an adjustment for ageing of buildings. Investors in ordinary shares also expect to achieve their long-term investment returns from dividend income and capital appreciation.

However, the nature of the long-term capital appreciation in shares and property is different. To begin with, there is the additional factor of retained profits which influences the long-term capital appreciation of ordinary shares.

Unfortunately, this is not widely understood, and as a result there are two incompatible views as to the nature of the long-term appreciation of ordinary shares.

The most widely held belief is that the underlying force is inflation. To a large extent this belief is based on the argument that in the long run share prices must exhibit much the same trend as company profits and dividends which, other things being equal, should be a stable proportion of the Gross Domestic Product and therefore move with inflation.

The opposite view, the less widely held, is that the long-term capital appreciation of ordinary shares has little to do with inflation. Writing in early 1972, Benjamin Graham identified profit retention rather than inflation as the prime source of earnings growth in US companies[9]:

"The cold figures demonstrate that all the large gain in the earnings of the [Dow Jones Index] unit in the past 20 years was due to a proportionately large growth of invested capital coming from reinvested profits. If inflation had operated as a separate favourable factor, its effect would have been to increase the 'value' of previously existing capital; this in turn should increase the rate of earnings on such old capital and therefore on the old and new capital combined. But nothing of the kind actually happened in the last 20 years, during which the wholesale price level has advanced nearly 40%."

The figures which follow show Australian, US and UK share price indices at yearly intervals (calendar year-end figures) from 1920 to 1990 inclusive using the same semi-logarithmic scale.

Australian All Ordinaries 5.4%   **US Dow Jones Industrial Averages 4.6%**

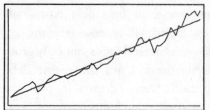 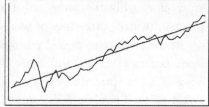

UK de Zoetes Equities 5.6%

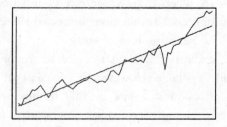

Over the 70-year period from 1920 to 1990, the average return on shareholders' funds for the Dow Jones Industrial Averages was 11.6% and the average payout ratio was 60%. Retained profits therefore averaged 40% of 11.6% or 4.6% per annum which is the same as the gradient of the calculated line of best fit.

In the period 1959/60 to 1977/78 data obtained from the Reserve Bank of Australia demonstrated that retained profits, as a proportion of shareholders' funds, averaged 3.9% per annum in respect of a group of companies known as the Reserve Bank All Industries Constant Group.

Based on this incomplete information one may perhaps expect share prices in all three countries to increase at around 4% per annum on account of retained profits. If inflation had been an additional factor the slopes of these lines would have been twice as steep — the slope would have been around 10% per annum in all cases instead of 5%. The fact that these slopes were closer to 4% bears out Graham's analysis rather than the more common belief of an inflation hedge. On the other hand the 'inflation hedge' belief is so widely held its fallacy needs to be explained.

If companies are to grow or maintain their scale of operation in real terms then their capital base must also grow. If the capital base does not grow at roughly the same rate then sooner or later debt ratios will prevent further borrowings or working capital will become deficient.

In the absence of capital raisings, shareholders' funds can only grow from retained profits and asset revaluations. Until the recent debt write-offs, the principal asset revaluations were increases in property holdings. In the case of US companies asset revaluations have not been permitted since the 1930s.

In Australia and the UK the situation is more complicated because companies periodically revalue their property assets. In the period 1970/71 to 1977/78, when the average rate of inflation in Australia was 10.7% per annum, asset revaluations increased shareholders' funds by an additional 2.7% per annum on average.

Unfortunately, extensive data on rates of return on shareholders' funds is not readily available. However, it appears that the long-term growth in share prices (if it keeps broadly in line with growth in shareholders' funds) is predominantly accounted for by profit retentions. If inflation is a factor influencing the long-term movements of share prices, its influence is only partial and in the case of US shares inflation may not be a factor at all.

Providing companies did not have to raise capital the inflation hedge argument would be quite satisfactory. Unfortunately, this is not the case and while the total dividend pool may keep pace with inflation (or the Gross Domestic Product), entitlement to part of this dividend stream passes to subscribers to new shares whenever companies raise fresh capital.

Consider the simple case of a company which pays out all its profits in dividends and which has no property assets. It has two classes of shareholders, class A shareholders who never take up entitlements to new issues and class B shareholders who always do. Let us suppose that earnings, dividends and shareholders' funds all grow at x% per annum. What happens to the dividends received by class A shareholders? Their dividend income will remain constant, so will the earnings per share and so will the net tangible assets per share. That is to say, their experience will follow the rate of retention of profits — in this case zero.

Alternatively, we could consider the situation in which there is no inflation and in which the company earned 10% on shareholders' funds and paid 60% in dividends. Here the company could afford to increase its business by 4% per annum in real terms without raising fresh capital. Consequently its dividends, earnings and net tangible assets per share would all increase at 4% per annum. Class A shareholders would enjoy a dividend stream increasing at 4% per annum and remain entitled to all of it. They would once again experience growth of 4% per annum — the retained profits as a percentage of shareholders' funds.

A second approach to the counter-inflationary virtues of ordinary shares is based on the premise that share prices should broadly move with inflation because their ownership represents a charge over real assets such as plant, equipment and stock. While stock, plant and equipment may be items which maintain their real value, they are not treated as real items under the historical cost accounting convention.

When senior management sits down to review the price for its companies' goods and services, this exercise is usually based on making a profit conventionally measured. These calculations rarely take into account the necessity of allowing for depreciation on plant at current replacement costs, nor the current cost of replacing stock sold.

For example, let us suppose a petrol retailer purchases his stock at a cost of 50 cents per litre and sells it at 55 cents per litre. Under normal accounting this represents a 'profit' of 5 cents per litre. Now let us suppose that the wholesale price has jumped to 60 cents per litre overnight. If he continues to sell his existing stock at 55 cents per litre he will have to pay 5 cents more per litre to replace his stock. By continuing to sell his stock at 55 cents he may be making an accounting profit, but in real terms he is making a loss and will eventually go bankrupt if this policy is persistently followed.

This point is well recognised in inflationary times when the subject of 'inflation accounting' becomes a popular topic. But it should be noted that product pricing (or profit planning) is generally pursued in money terms and stewardship of shareholders' funds is reported in money terms.

This discussion necessarily involves complex accounting concepts. Unfortunately the effect of inflation on ordinary shares is too important a topic to be ignored and further discussion appears in Chapter 8. At the very least it should be noted that the widely held belief that there is some nexus between share prices and inflation in the long run is not borne out in the available data.

FORECASTING SECTORAL RETURNS — AN EXERCISE IN COMMERCIAL ASTROLOGY?

Let us now gaze into a crystal ball to see if it is possible to estimate the likely long-term returns from cash, property and ordinary shares, assuming typical results and that investments are made at 'average' prices. To do this we need first to hazard a guess at the likely long-term rate of inflation — say 4% to pull a figure out of the hat — and know the tax rate of the investor — say 30%.

➤ *Cash investments* should return somewhat in excess of the rate of inflation — say 7% per annum or 5% after tax.

➤ *Property* should return 6% real or 10% in money terms. The tax on capital gains should not be significant and 30% tax on the income component (6%) will reduce the return by 2% per annum. Thus the net return is 4% real or 8% in money terms.

➤ *Ordinary shares* should return a dividend of 4% plus long-term capital growth of 5% — made up of 4% retained profits plus 1% from partial movement with inflation. As this is roughly the same as the rate of inflation, capital gains taxes should not be significant. The total return is therefore 9% gross. This return must be adjusted for imputation credits by adding back the imputed taxes of approximately 60% of the dividend (2.5%) and then deducting tax at the rate of 30% from the combined dividend and imputed tax of 6.5% (2.0%). The total return from ordinary shares is therefore projected at 9.5% after tax in money terms or 5.5% in real terms.

It is difficult to assess the long-term effect of the introduction of dividend imputation. In the past, changes in company tax rates appear to have been passed on. Dividend imputation is different because it affects the tax payable by shareholders on their investments rather than having a direct effect on companies themselves. On the other hand, dividend imputation considerably increases the value of dividends to shareholders. In the future a lower level of corporate profitability may emerge as the acceptable 'norm'. For this reason, a safety margin should be built into the use of the 'pre-imputation' record to make future projections.

On a directly comparable basis the projected long-term returns from cash, property and ordinary shares net of tax (and assuming investments are purchased and sold at reasonable prices) are therefore 5%, 8% and 9.5% per annum respectively, but the figure of 9.5% per annum for shares should possibly be shaved a little to allow for the long-term effect of dividend imputation.

INTERNATIONAL EQUITY INVESTMENT

While much the same principles, coupled with foreign exchange considerations, apply to foreign shares, there are a number of important accounting and taxation differences.

Generally speaking, the accounting procedures in the UK, USA, Canada and New Zealand are similar to those applying in Australia, but there are important differences. For example, in the USA, property assets are not written up periodically and there is widespread use of last-in-first-out accounting for cost-of-goods-sold. Australian residents are not usually subject to foreign capital gains taxes but dividend payments are usually subject to the deduction of withholding tax. This can usually be deducted from the Australian liability but there is no imputation benefit. There is thus a substantial bias in favour of Australian residents investing in Australian companies.

There are also pitfalls for the unwary such as the Foreign Investment Fund legislation and the capital gains liability incurred on 'traditional' bonus share issues. Consequently, a degree of sophistication is required for anyone contemplating foreign investment.

These problems are not so severe for portfolios subject to low rates of tax such as superannuation funds, but taxpayers with high marginal rates of tax should be wary of the tax consequences of foreign investment. Taxation of international income is a complex business involving international double taxation treaties as well as specialised aspects of Australian law. In consequence, the necessary taxation advice relating to overseas investment may cost a little more.

Other things being equal, and using the assumptions of our previous crystal ball, the long-term return from foreign equities will be 8% gross but unless foreign dividends give rise to an imputation credit, the net return will be only 6.8% which is almost 3% per annum net less than the return from a comparable local portfolio.

Portfolio investment in overseas shares, under the tax regime existing in 1997, is therefore undertaken with the long-term odds stacked against Australian residents. Consequently, such investors operating internationally need to be doing so for the benefit of diversification, or for some other reason which will overcome these disadvantages.

Chapter 4

Investment Objectives and Strategy; Formulation, Implementation and Supervision

INTERDEPENDENCE OF INVESTMENT OBJECTIVES AND RISK

IN THE PREVIOUS chapter, the characteristics of different investments were discussed. This provided some indication as to the sort of investment return that it is possible to achieve. The next step is to ascertain the requirements of the investor and then try to match these requirements with suitable investments.

Recent legislation has formalised the process of formulating objectives for superannuation funds in Australia.[1] While there is no need for investors not subject to these requirements to follow them, adopting the process may still be helpful.

As we have already seen, investment risk depends on the circumstances and objectives of the investor as well as the investment portfolio. However, feasible investment results, and therefore realistic investment objectives, also depend on the risk-tolerance of the investor.

This suggests that the discussion of risk and objectives inevitably becomes a circular argument. Knowledge of the objectives is necessary to define risk, but consideration of risk-tolerance is important in establishing objectives. Failure to consider investments and investors' requirements together can lead to a serious mismatch of assets and liabilities.

Mismatches of assets and liabilities or investments and investors' requirements can occur in numerous ways.

A common mismatch is the purchase of shares using funds which should be set aside to meet short-term obligations or borrowing funds at call for property development or share trading. An extreme example of this occurred in the case of Mineral Securities Australia Ltd at the time of the Poseidon boom.[2] An institutional investor at the time recalled:[3]

> "*Mineral Securities had some genuine mining operations, but began to make large profits from share trading. The Australian financial world generally held as high an opinion of the company as it did of itself, and worthy companies lent it large sums of money without any security at all.*
>
> "*I remember reading a draft prospectus for a new issue of preference shares by the company. All was routine until the third page where it was reported that the company's affairs had not materially altered since the last annual report, except that assets had increased by the purchase of more than $30,000,000 worth of mining shares, while liabilities in the form of short term loans (mainly loans at call) had increased by the same amount.*
>
> "*Unable to believe my eyes, I telephoned the brokers who assured me that all was well, the shares purchased were in very good companies!*"

Shortly thereafter, Mineral Securities was placed in liquidation. In *Two Centuries of Panic*, Trevor Sykes described how without some bold action from the then Bank of New South Wales and reassuring noises from the Reserve Bank, the liquidation could have taken a great deal of the short-term money market and the broking community with it.[4]

A less common mismatch occurs when funds are borrowed in foreign currency to finance the purchase (or retention) of assets usually valued or traded in another currency. Borrowing money is usually risky in itself as it implies gearing of assets, but as foreign currency borrowers who have lost their farms, houses and businesses have discovered, borrowing can be even more risky if borrowers are subject to a currency mismatch between their assets and liabilities. Let us suppose a farmer borrowed (say) $US 100,000 when the exchange rate was $A1 = $US 1.50 — as was the case in 1972. If this loan was still outstanding then the debt would still be $US 100,000 but at current exchange rates the amount owing in Australian dollars would have risen from approximately $A 67,000 in 1972 to $A 150,000 in 1997 as a result of exchange rate movements between the Australian and US dollars. The relative movements of some of the other currencies have been more dramatic.

The lessons of these mismatches is that they can be highly speculative. An investment policy which is temporarily mismatched carries some risk of disaster. If a seriously mismatched policy is persistently pursued it will more likely be a question of when rather than whether insolvency occurs.

Individual investors and superannuation trustees who do not borrow to invest may question the relevance of the Mineral Securities debacle to their own circumstances. One lesson of this episode is the need to be alert to circumstances in which investments are subject to this form of collapse.

In the case of Mineral Securities, mining shares were not a suitable investment for a company with substantial loan capital repayable at call because a decline in the market could lead to a situation where outstanding loans exceeded the current value of their portfolio. But what would happen if funds were repayable at short notice and the assets could not be sold quickly?

Unlisted property trusts were a popular investment for retirees in the late 1980s. However, their structure contained a flaw which proved to be fatal – if a majority of investors wished their units redeemed, it eventually became necessary to sell some of the underlying property and if other unlisted trusts were in the same position sales at reasonable prices became impossible. Here, one of the investment requirements of the unlisted property trust itself — liquidity to meet unit-holder redemptions — could not be matched by the type of assets they intended to buy.

People involved at the time will recall the Australian Securities Commission's requirement for adequate buy-back arrangements. As things turned out, these arrangements were inadequate to cope with the crisis, and a number of bank subsidiaries failed to live up to investors' expectations in this respect. Were these expectations not influenced by the (deliberately publicised) parentage of management companies and a semi-official prescription for buy-back arrangements?

While mismatches of currency (foreign loans) and liquidity (unlisted property trusts) can be spectacular in their aftermath, there can be other forms of mismatch which can be just as devastating, but over a longer period of time. One requirement is the need of the majority of private investors for an income which keeps pace with inflation — bearing in mind the fact that Australian currency has lost 98% of its purchasing power this century.

A popular catchcry in the investment industry is maximisation of net return — subject of course to an acceptable degree of risk (whatever that means). But is this tenable? If investors have enough assets to meet their requirements, why should they incur any risks trying to make money they do not need? If superannuation funds are sufficiently financial to meet their members' needs (and employers are happy to meet the contributions required by this assessment) whose interests are trustees serving in seeking to maximise return?

It is nevertheless true that maximising investment returns will minimise the contributions required to reach either a defined or desired level of benefits and this approach has particular interest for corporations funding defined benefit schemes. However, corporate life may be risky enough for employees as it is without assuming additional risks with superannuation investments. Any widespread downturn in corporate fortunes is very likely to be reflected in stock markets while simultaneously prompting payment of retrenchment and 'early retirement' benefits.

This suggests that maximisation of returns may only be tenable when risk does not matter and only contemplated with surplus assets. If a risky policy is pursued as part of an attempt to reach this position cheaply or prematurely, then risk is possibly being assumed by investors who cannot afford it or whose security may be jeopardised in periods of corporate malaise when security of benefits is most likely to be needed.

While no-one invests with the intention of losing money, the investor needs a clearer idea of investment objectives than a vague intention of making money. For example, there is a considerable difference between saving for a holiday in six months' time, and putting money aside to provide a retirement income.

All investments involve risk of one sort or another, even if it is the unthinkable proposition of government default — bearing in mind perhaps that effective default as a result of inflation is almost inevitable.

Consequently, the purpose of any savings or investment program will often severely limit the available options. The purpose of the investment is just one of a number of factors which need to be taken into account in determining an acceptable level of risk.

As risk cannot be defined in isolation from investors' objectives let us now consider the requirements of a variety of investors and then return to the meaning of risk.

THE REQUIREMENTS OF PRIVATE INDIVIDUALS

The investment requirements of private individuals are not usually subject to any legal constraints, but they can be quite complicated because of the myriad issues which need to be taken into account. Furthermore, the purpose often changes with age, business success or failure, marital status and other personal circumstances.

The implications of age and (lack of) employment status are limiting factors which are not always appreciated by younger people who sometimes see financial conservatism as a sign of approaching senility, rather than an attitude which is essential for survival. 'Starting again' with nothing but enthusiasm is not a financial impossibility under the age of 40, but the difficulty increases with age. An investor who loses everything at 40 is in a vastly different position to someone who becomes destitute in retirement at age 70.

Self-Funded Retirees

On retirement, many of the issues facing younger people with dependants cease to apply and investment can become more focused on the principal purpose of generating enough money to support an acquired lifestyle.

Those whose wealth substantially exceeds their requirements can afford to squander some of it. However, very few people are in this position and the majority of self-funded retirees need to be careful, both with their investments and their budgets.

A psychological factor affecting retirees is the need for peace of mind which arises from a recognition of their vulnerable status if problems emerge. Accordingly, the basic requirements of self-funded retirees are straightforward even if the investment strategy to meet these needs is not. These requirements are:

(a) An income which is adequate and keeps pace with inflation, and

(b) A sense of security – implying non-volatile investments and a conservative choice of individual assets.

The latter requirement will depend a great deal on the personality and attitudes of the person concerned.

Youthful Investors

From a financial point of view there is probably not much point in people under 35 with typical family and mortgage commitments saving large amounts of money outside of superannuation without first reducing their mortgage commitments. Interest paid on home mortgages by Australian residents is not usually a tax-deductible expense. This makes it difficult to achieve an after-tax return which exceeds the highly secure return available by simply reducing the amount outstanding under a mortgage.

According to this argument, savings should be directed towards paying off a non-deductible debt before any other voluntary investments are considered. There are, however, two important non-taxation considerations to bear in mind.

First, those who do not venture into the stock market until they retire have deprived themselves of the years of experience necessary to invest safely at a later date. The experience achieved in 30 years involvement prior to retirement will not only be invaluable, it may also exceed the experience of those offering investment advice to fellow retirees in due course. As Gerald Loeb, a well known Wall Street 'legend', wrote 40 years ago:[5]

> "The only way to begin is to learn by doing. Here lies the greatest handicap of most investors. They have no experience. And unfortunately, most of them go for advice to others who either have had no experience or have had enough to induce them to leave markets alone and concentrate on brokerage or advisory or statistical work".

[Ouch!]

Despite the theoretical perfection of the taxation argument, there is a second reason for not giving top priority to the discharge of the typical home mortgage. The psychological effect of a 'clear title' on the family home seems to be such a novel experience for some people that it can invoke a passion for a bigger house with a new mortgage — and an increased cost of living. In effect, this involves the accumulation of 'income-consuming' real estate beyond personal requirements which may prove to be a real burden at a later stage.

If the purpose of discharging debt is to achieve a tax position from which serious investment is proposed, there is no point in pursuing this course if, when the mortgage is discharged, the owners decide to 'trade-up'.

Therefore it would seem sensible to be more flexible than tax considerations alone would dictate, provided any large personal debts are first reduced to manageable proportions before making significant stock market investments. If this is not done then the investor is, in effect, operating in the stock market on borrowed funds.

If the most important aspect of 'youthful' investment is the acquisition of experience, then investment activities could be directed to this end at first. In *The Battle for Investment Survival*, Gerald Loeb advances some interesting ideas for 'experience investing'.[6] He suggests the establishment of a small experience fund all invested initially in one stock. This sort of activity should force the beginner to:

> "... a decision whether to keep [a stock], take a loss of profit, or exchange it for another. [This] is quite different, and many times more valuable in teaching market technique, than the imaginary 'paper transactions' in which tyros indulge. The latter are completely lacking in testing the investors' psychological reactions stemming from such important factors as fear of loss, or greed for more gain."

Mid-Life Rollovers

The payment of financial 'packages' on retrenchment and 'voluntary' early retirement in the 40 to 50 age group has become a common feature of Australian commercial life. For tax reasons, most of these funds need to remain within the superannuation system in 'rollover' funds, although the individuals concerned often have a wide choice of funds including private 'excluded funds' of which they are the sole member.

There are many stories about insomnia amongst people who were retrenched and who plunged their 'package' into the stock market. Buying shares (directly or indirectly) may or may not have been sound advice from a financial point of view, but someone who is in a weak psychological state as a result of being retrenched may be easily worried by the stock market. This is not a suitable state of mind in which to make investment decisions. Also it distracts from the more important task of finding a job.

Investors whose investment activities prevent a good night's sleep may find it preferable to treat the cause of the problem (conducting investment activities for which they are psychologically unsuited) rather than attempt to relieve the symptoms with pills.

After people in this situation have sorted out their employment problems, they will need to seek a more permanent home for their rollover funds. This means that the initial requirements of the majority of investors in this predicament are secure, liquid and non-volatile investments. The rate of return becomes a factor once re-employed, but is a secondary consideration until this is achieved.

Although they are not strictly investment matters, there should be two other items on the financial risk check-list for would-be investors in these age groups. They are insurance (life, disability and medical — it is strange how many people insure their house but forget to insure their life) and some sort of 'emergency fund' consisting of (say) six months' basic living expenses held on deposit with a bank, cash management trust or comparable institution.

People employed by large organisations are often provided with life insurance as part of their superannuation arrangements. Sometimes this cover is portable, but not always and in any event the 'old' cover usually ceases on departure from a fund. Portability of life cover is worth consideration and investigation, particularly for anyone who is not in excellent health.

THE REQUIREMENTS OF DEFINED CONTRIBUTION OR ACCUMULATION SUPERANNUATION FUNDS

Superannuation funds in Australia fall into two main types. A declining number of large companies sponsor *defined benefit* or *final salary* funds with retirement benefits based on years of service and salary in the last few years prior to retirement. By contrast, *defined contribution* or *accumulation funds* usually receive a regular percentage of members' salary or wages and the end benefit depends directly on the investment results.

The principal purpose of both types of funds is to accumulate funds from members and/or their employers throughout their working life, invest them until the member retires and then provide the members with retirement benefits. If these benefits are not taken in pension form, the member will then need to invest the proceeds to produce an income.

To a significant extent superannuation is now compulsory and, from the members' point of view, money paid into a superannuation fund on their behalf is increasingly seen as their money especially when it is paid into a fund outside their employer's control.

If members were saving the money themselves and investing it themselves (in a tax-sheltered environment until they retired) and then living on the income after they retired, the specification of investment objectives would be relatively simple — generating an asset base which produces an inflation-proof income in retirement. If there are safe ways of achieving this result, there is no benefit in taking unnecessary risks. If, on the other hand, safe investments will leave a small shortfall, it might be preferable for prospective retirees to slightly increase the contributions while working rather than taking investment risks in an attempt to achieve adequate retirement benefits from inadequate savings.

There is, therefore, a long-term investment program underneath the legal structures within which members' benefits are held while they are in the workforce. Why then, are trustees of accumulation funds — presumably under the actual or perceived pressure of members — so concerned about volatility?

For the time being, let us assume that it is appropriate for such funds to hold (say) 40% in ordinary shares. Members who retire when stock and/or bond markets are depressed should then take their benefit and reinvest in much the same way at depressed prices. Conversely, if the market is overpriced members' benefits will have been inflated but the prices of some of the assets they need to buy will also be inflated. There is therefore a hedge against inflated or depressed markets provided the underlying assets follow the member from one structure to the next. Should greater use be made of 'transfer *in specie*' arrangements, thereby setting up retirees with a professionally-selected portfolio and avoiding most transaction costs?

Unfortunately, this may be another example where emotion over-rules logic in the investment world. Members of funds, and their trustees under actual or perceived member pressure, are usually looking for three things:

(a) An investment return which exceeds inflation — often on a three-year rolling basis.

(b) Negative yearly returns less than once every (say) 10 years.

(c) Results which are at least as good as the average achieved by similar professionally managed funds.

The requirement for negative returns no more than once in every (say) 10 years is a popular objective because it appears to protect members from major declines in their benefits. There will be times when price declines happen and, when they do, the extent of the decline and their overall effect on a portfolio is more important than their frequency. For example, in a 10-year period, two minor declines of (say) 5% might be tolerable, but one substantial decline of (say) 30% may not be acceptable.

In this respect, specifying the maximum frequency of negative returns is inadequate without the first objective of requiring rolling three-year returns in excess of inflation. As an expression of conservatism, requiring three-year rolling returns in excess of inflation may carry an implicit requirement for infrequent negative returns which is stronger than the popular explicit objective.

In consequence, the objective which matters most is the first requirement of achieving a return in excess of the rate of inflation — although the term should be longer, because this is the underlying need of members. In practice, however, the objective which attracts the greatest attention is achieving a competitive return.

This desire for a competitive return is nothing new. As Keynes pointed out in 1935, it is an inevitable consequence of the way in which the professional market has operated for decades.[7] By making increasing use of professional management firms and, by taking keen interest in their investment performance, rather than the soundness of their overall strategy, market assessment and implementation, trustees are being drawn into the same 'performance' game as professional money managers. On this subject, Keynes wrote:[8]

"The practice, usually considered prudent, by which an investment trust or an insurance office frequently calculates not only the income from its

investment portfolio but also its capital valuation in the market, may also tend to direct too much attention to short-term fluctuations in the latter."

If the return from Fund A is 10% when the return from Fund B is 20%, members of Fund A will be asking why they did not do as well as their friends in Fund B, particularly if Fund B is more typical of the 'average' fund. However, if Fund A declines 10% and the more typical Fund B declines by 20%, members of Fund B will be reassured by being part of the herd with similar results. Furthermore, the managers of Fund A may, in effect be accused of taking excessive 'risk' — the 'risk' of assessing the herd to be wrong and taking a contrarian stance.

As far as these influences on fund managers and trustees are concerned, Keynes offered the following advice:[9]

"Worldly wisdom teaches that it is better to fail conventionally than to succeed unconventionally."

Considering the visibility of the investment results of accumulation schemes and the increasing move towards 'member choice' it seems inevitable that trustees who wish to keep their members will be reduced to seeking 'average' results — irrespective of their assessment of the long-term return from various investment options. Under the influence of investment performance calculations and surveys, rule of the mob has taken over!

For those who wish to exclude themselves from this potential crowd madness, the option of establishing a private or 'excluded' superannuation fund is sometimes available — at some cost.

THE REQUIREMENTS OF FINAL SALARY OR DEFINED BENEFIT SCHEMES

Company-sponsored defined benefit schemes are in a slightly different position to accumulation schemes because, in normal circumstances, the investment return affects the cost to the employer more than members' benefits.

It is often thought that large corporate pension funds are fairly free of any liquidity and volatility considerations on the grounds that the average age of the members is 35 years and they will all be receiving pensions based on their salary and service with the company.

Unfortunately, there are two very significant contingencies which have a bearing on the requirements for liquidity and stability of investment returns. First, there is always the risk of extensive retrenchments when the economy is depressed and when share and property prices are also likely to be depressed. The departure of a significant proportion of the fund membership on reasonably generous terms when markets are depressed would then have a leveraged effect on the security of the remaining members of the fund. Secondly, most pension funds usually permit full or partial commutation into a lump sum.

One would think that when offered what they generally need — an indexed income for the rest of their life — retirees would welcome the chance of a couple of decades post-retirement free of financial worries. Despite the fact that the majority of people in this position have no experience in handling such sums, particularly when they can ill-afford mistakes, they usually prefer to commute as much of their pensions as possible into lump sums.

From the point of view of the fund, this creates an irregular incidence of large payouts instead of a regular transition from contributor to pensioner.

In addition to requirements based on the circumstances of the fund, there may be additional reasons for avoiding volatile investments as a result of the vested benefit and accrued benefit ratios imposed under Australian legislation.[10] If these ratios are not exceeded by a healthy margin, then the investment strategy may be very restrained.

Assuming, for the moment, that these legislated ratio requirements are not a consideration, what are the requirements of a company-sponsored defined benefit scheme? From the discussion it would appear that as benefits are based on salaries, the principal requirement is for investments which can be relied upon to produce a long-term return in excess of the rate of inflation — irrespective of what inflation turns out to be.

The next requirement is to accumulate assets which will not be unduly affected by an unexpected economic downturn because this would be likely to trigger the need for benefit payments. If the market value of the assets of the fund is simultaneously depressed, this could jeopardise the security of the benefits of ongoing members.

At present, conventional wisdom suggests that ordinary shares will more or less meet these requirements as well as minimising the cost to the employer. Typically 60% of the assets of such funds in Australia in

1997 are invested in ordinary shares; 40% Australian, 20% offshore. This conventional wisdom is based on three partially implicit assumptions:

(a) Ordinary shares will produce the greatest rate of return because they are rationally priced in such a way that the investor obtains a 'risk premium' for investing in volatile assets

(b) Shares provide a long-term hedge against inflation and if inflation turns out higher than currently anticipated then the return from ordinary shares will be correspondingly higher than current projections

(c) Should there be an unexpected change in the employer's fortunes requiring wholesale retrenchments, the economic circumstances will not otherwise affect the financial position of the fund.

In the previous chapter the relationship between inflation and ordinary shares was discussed at some length. The idea of a nexus between long-term returns on shares and inflation is probably false and the most that can be said is that it is unproven. However, irrespective of the long-term merits of shares as an inflation hedge, an unexpected rise in inflation in the short term will almost certainly be accompanied by a rise in interest rates, lower corporate profitability and lower price/earnings ratios to boot.

At the same time, the inflation-linked liabilities of final salary schemes will be increasing faster than anticipated. **If a fund is heavily invested in shares, the overall short-term consequence of an unexpected increase in inflation is therefore likely to be a deterioration of the fund's financial position on both sides of the balance sheet.**

Let us briefly consider the suitability of two other major asset classes for defined benefit/final salary funds. If inflation rises then interest rates will probably rise as well — leading to a simultaneous escalation in liabilities, rises in interest rates and declines in long-term bond prices. This suggests that short-term fixed-interest securities may be a suitable investment but long-term fixed-interest securities may not. In these circumstances of rising interest rates, there may be an increased need for liquidity to meet benefit payments.

While property may provide a long-term hedge against inflation, an increase in inflation and interest rates will probably also see a decline in property prices and also a decline in the prices of units in listed property trusts. However, the price decline is likely to be smaller than the effect of an increase in interest rates on ordinary shares.

This suggests that the bulk of defined benefit/final salary funds might be more appropriately invested with more than 50% in short-term fixed-interest securities and property rather than shares — and not the other way around.

SPECIALISED INSTITUTIONAL REQUIREMENTS

The investment requirements of organisations such as life offices, (general) insurance companies, friendly societies, banks, building societies and credit unions tend to be quite specialised and these such organisations are usually well staffed and/or advised on such matters. Nevertheless, less sophisticated investors using (say) building societies may find it helpful to give some thought to the way in which the organisation handles funds entrusted to its care.

The underlying principle still applies to these organisations — investments should be suitable after taking into account the purpose of the investment, any legal constraints and any liabilities for which the investment is set aside. If these requirements are not met, then depositors may not have access to their funds as they were led to expect.

To give an example, building societies normally accept deposits from the public repayable at short notice. Consequently their basic investment requirements are liquidity (because their liabilities are at short notice), security (because they are non-profit organisations with modest reserves and not much margin for error) and negligible volatility (because their depositors do not expect the capital value of their deposits to fluctuate).

To some extent two of these requirements (low volatility and high security) are met by mortgages on owner-occupied residential property subject to rigorous lending requirements. In practice, the third requirement is usually met by holding a substantial proportion of assets in high quality short-dated bank and government paper.

Without a ready secondary market in mortgages (to provide liquidity for the whole portfolio) this policy cannot be entirely satisfactory. A secondary mortgage market is developing, but it will take some time before it becomes sufficiently liquid to provide building societies with complete liquidity. However, when serious financial problems emerge within building societies they have usually been due to management ignoring the importance of security and low volatility. In the end, liquidity becomes a problem but when it does it is usually the result of a 'run' caused by doubts about the security of the underlying mortgage assets rather than their lack of liquidity.

One other form of matching is that required by specialised fixed-interest funds established for the payment of fixed or indexed annuities. In this case the maturity pattern of the assets has to be chosen so that the ability of the portfolio to meet payments to annuitants is not affected by fluctuations in interest rates. This is a mathematical problem which has limited interest outside a relatively small circle of specialists.[11]

'CAPITAL STABLE' FUNDS AND SAVINGS SCHEMES

A number of superannuation funds are run as savings schemes — these are defined contribution or accumulation arrangements where the members are given some form of guarantee or assurance that the rate of return in any financial year will not be negative.

There are two ways of achieving this non-negative return. The first is to restrict the underlying investments to stable, secure and liquid assets. The second is to build up reserves to permit a more adventurous investment policy.

After the stock market crash of 1987, packaged financial products offering capital stability were quite popular. This popularity was increased considerably when some of the funds had accumulated large reserves over a number of years and above average returns could be offered to prospective members.

The next chapter contains a discussion of corporate behaviour and the conflict between business growth and investors. On some occasions it appears that business growth has been pursued for its own sake and in this respect returns to investors can be a means to an end rather than an end in themselves. In this ethical environment, members of funds with accumulated reserves — for which they have paid — may see their reserves being used to attract new business rather than increase the returns allocated to themselves.

There are therefore two questions which need to be addressed. First, what is an appropriate investment policy when capital guarantees are provided and reserves are held to permit a more liberal investment policy? Second, should a member of the public join a 'capital guaranteed' fund which accumulates reserves to underwrite a mismatched investment policy?

An important consideration in answering the second question is the soundness (or otherwise) of the investment policy of the fund. Investors contemplating participation in 'capital guaranteed' funds should therefore understand, from the point of view of the fund, the policy issues involved.

If capital guarantees are provided there is a natural desire to increase the long-term performance of the fund by investing in ordinary shares and property. Clearly this is quite unsound if the investors are expecting a return on their money which will always be positive unless reserves are held to absorb losses in bad years. Consequently, some surplus must be created by withholding some income each year until a more adventurous policy can be sustained.

Let us suppose that all goes well and reserves are built up. What happens then? If the accumulated reserves of previous cohorts are used to attract new investors then the 'old' cohorts of investors, which have suffered from some of their money being held back in the past, are passing the enjoyment of the surpluses to a new cohort of investors. On the other hand, if things go badly, the fund will not attract new members and cushion the blow for 'old' cohorts.

Investors in 'capital guaranteed' or 'capital stable' schemes where the underwriting institution conducts a mismatched investment policy may therefore be carrying most of the risk in bad years and giving up much of the reward in good ones. If things go badly their returns will be very low, and if things go well profits will be retained to build up reserves. Their enjoyment of the accumulated reserves may be severely diluted if such reserves are used to attract new investors. In so far as 'regulated' superannuation funds are concerned, there are now considerable restrictions on the accumulation of undistributed reserves.

From time to time it has been possible to invest in funds with accumulated reserves from which there will be immediate benefit to new investors at the expense of existing investors. Such opportunities tend to be actively promoted when they exist. It is a way of benefiting from reserves for which other people have paid. From a financial point of view this may be quite attractive provided a penalty-free exit is planned as soon as the benefit has been received, but there are moral issues in pursuing this course which may not appeal to everybody.

Finally, how should a 'capital guaranteed' fund invest in ordinary shares and/or property, if at all?

At first glance this investment strategy may seem reasonable. Reserves can be accumulated against future losses provided they are big enough to cover any possible losses. However, attempts to devise an appropriate formula quickly uncover some deep-rooted and far-reaching complexities in this approach. Let us say that the trustees of a superannuation fund agree to an unrestricted investment policy provided there are sufficient reserves to cover a 50% decline in the equity portfolio. Let us now suppose that the fund is significantly invested in shares and property trusts and the market value of these assets has just fallen by 25%. A large proportion of the shares held by the fund will now need to be sold to restore the 50% reserve margin.

The dangers of the situation become apparent when it is recognised that if such funds are popular there will be a large number of funds in a similar position and a widespread attempt to restore solvency reserves could lead to massive sell-off or 'stock market melt down' and/or widespread instability. It therefore seems unwise to adopt a mismatched policy in 'capital guaranteed' funds, notwithstanding the existence of reasonable reserves, particularly if the practice is popular.

An institutional investment manager, actively involved in these problems, drew attention to the dangers to the financial system as a whole by dominant market funds holding significant equity exposures when the investors were expecting 'always positive' returns:[12]

> "In the long run, as industry accumulation funds grow in size, they will become dominant players in the markets. They will not be able to get rid of their risks, because there will not be enough risk-takers to accept the other side of the transactions (unless extremely high prices are paid).

> "There is only one long-term solution which allows these funds to hold risky assets, and that is for the risks to be passed back to the members themselves – not necessarily all of them, but enough of them to create a stable financial environment ..."

The old problem of interest rates and bond prices moving in opposite directions makes this problem just as applicable to 'capital guaranteed' funds which invest in long-dated fixed-interest securities. The comments about mismatching, and the advisability of investing in such funds also apply to investment pools restricted to fixed-interest investment. In fixed-interest pools restricted to short-term assets such as cash management trusts these problems will be barely noticeable, but they still occur.

Someone who inherits the management of a mismatched fund with substantial reserves is confronted with an ethical dilemma. Should the fund be returned to a matched position and the profits distributed to investors? It is not difficult to understand the temptation of using reserves to underwrite new business which dilutes the interests of existing investors. But should it be possible for the business interests of a fund manager or life office to prevail over the financial interest of an investor?

In the absence of statutory prevention, investors should question the advisability of participating in funds which maintain reserves to 'smooth' investment results — particularly if the chosen fund is open to the public at large. Funds can seek security or accept risk as the price for what is expected to be a higher long-term return. Trying to have an each-way bet jeopardises both objectives.

WHAT IS RISK?

The examples discussed so far suggest that investment risk for long-term investors is, generally speaking, the chance of not achieving a rate of return modestly in excess of inflation. If this is achieved then investors will be able to accumulate sufficient assets during their working lives which then can be used to produce an adequate income in retirement.

The fact that the underlying assets are held in a variety of different structures, be they superannuation funds, rollover funds, allocated pension funds or in the investor's own name is only a superficial part of the process and would be unnecessary if it were not for the taxation incentives and other advantages of superannuation arrangements.

However, the existence of these custodial intermediaries introduces a new series of objectives and pressures. Members of funds look to trustees for investment results and the trustees, not unreasonably, see themselves as being responsible for the funds while they are under their custody — the broader perspective and very long-term nature of the members' underlying needs are often hidden beneath all the paperwork, government regulation and conflicting perceptions.

The 1934 edition of *Security Analysis* gave a definition of investment which is worth repeating:[13]

> *"An investment operation is one which upon thorough analysis promises safety of principal and an adequate return. Operations not meeting these requirements are speculative."*

For the vast majority of superannuation fund members, an adequate return is one which can be expected to exceed inflation in the long run by a modest margin. One of the disadvantages of superannuation investment as it is often practised today is that, under the pressure for performance and/or always positive results, this underlying requirement has been almost forgotten.

While the first aspect of risk is principally due to mismatches between investors' requirements and the investments held to meet these objectives, a second aspect relates to risks inherent in the investments themselves. For example, a portfolio of (say) 15 industrial stocks in different industries with much the same amount invested in each, is likely to be a great deal less risky than a portfolio of (say) four stocks in the mining industry.

The understanding of investment risk has not been helped by those disciples of Modern Portfolio Theory who call volatility risk. Indeed, the confusion of risk and volatility has almost become official and, in the process, performing mathematical calculations has become a substitute for thought. Consider for example this quotation which appeared in a book published by The Association of Superannuation Funds of Australia in 1992:[14]

> *"In terms of their risk levels, property investments come in after fixed-interest investments, but before equities. That is, they are more volatile than fixed-interest investments, but over the longer term, have been less volatile than shares."*

The existence of a ready market such as an organised stock exchange provides genuine investors with the option of increasing or reducing their holding at the prevailing price. The market is the servant of the genuine investor, it exists for the investor's participation, observation or amusement as the investor sees fit. Once investors take their idea of value from market prices or their idea of risk from price fluctuations, then the market has become a master rather than a servant.

There are a number of commonsense reasons why fixed-interest securities, property and ordinary shares should be ranked in that order of risk. Notwithstanding the confusion between risk and volatility, the relative ranking of these three asset classes therefore seems generally correct even if the reasoning is not. However, this ranking may not apply to all investors. We have already seen the way holding fixed-interest investments rather than shares creates a business risk for professional investors. Risk therefore partly depends on the objectives and any specific requirements of the investor as well as those inherent in the assets themselves.

One final aspect of risk concerns knowledge and experience. An investor operating in unknown fields is incurring the risk of ignorance. To quote Warren Buffett:[15]

> "What an investor needs is the ability to correctly evaluate selected businesses. Note that word selected: You don't have to be an expert on every company, or even many. You only have to be able to evaluate companies within your circle of competence. The size of that circle is not very important; knowing its boundaries, however, is vital."

This discussion demonstrates that risk cannot be accurately measured by using the (standard deviation of) volatility of investment results. Irrespective of the validity of Modern Portfolio Theory, there are far too many other factors to be considered. For this reason risk is essentially a qualitative judgement; at best it can be assessed, accurate enumeration could be misleading.

STRATEGIC ASSET ALLOCATION

The private investor who starts buying a few shares at the age of 25 and who has accumulated a portfolio by the age of 60 will probably have bought shares whenever he or she had some money to spare. Sales would have been rare and the timing of purchases would have been dictated by the availability of funds rather than attractiveness of the market at the time.

This bottom-up approach is very haphazard. It suffers from the disadvantage that the investor will most likely have spare funds to invest when a majority of investors are in a similar position and the stock market is buoyant. Consequently, the average cost under this approach will probably be higher than it should be.

Trustees of a superannuation fund will normally adopt a more formal procedure than this. At the very least they will need to meet and decide the maximum and minimum proportions of a fund which can be invested in the principal asset classes — shares, property, fixed-interest securities, listed property trusts, overseas equities, etc.

Establishing such asset allocation limits (for want of a better term) in the context of the investor's objectives and the general features of the different asset classes is perhaps the first step in controlling the overall risk of an investment operation. It would be normal for trustees of large superannuation funds to seek independent advice on this matter.

While this top-down approach may be a little foreign to value investors, they too would derive some benefit from using this approach to set limits as to the maximum proportion of their portfolio to be held in any one asset class.

Let us therefore consider the merits of the principal asset classes — cash, property and shares — in relation to some of the objectives discussed earlier.

A long-term return which exceeds inflation

The only asset classes which we can be reasonably sure of meeting this requirement in the long run are property and indexed government bonds. In the short term, there may be some merit in the view that should inflation rise, interest rates will also rise thereby enabling a portfolio of cash, property and indexed bonds to meet this requirement.

For reasons discussed at length in the previous chapter, shares do not generally meet this requirement — contrary to popular opinion. However, there would be some diversification merit in holding some shares; but if shares were to dominate the portfolio, an unexpected rise in inflation could jeopardise the long-term objective.

While the inflationary protection of local shares is doubtful, there may be more merit in investing in offshore assets as a hedge against inflation, particularly high inflation, on the premise that such inflation will tend to be reflected in currency depreciation in due course — other things being equal.

Maximum long-term return, subject to a specified limit on volatility *[Note the use of the word volatility and not risk!]*

For reasons already discussed in the previous chapter, which will be considered again in Chapter 8, a willingness to invest predominantly in ordinary shares is required because this asset class should, on average, produce the best long-term results.

However, this does not mean that the maximum proportion set aside for ordinary shares should become the minimum as well.

While pursuing a 'maximum long-term return strategy' it would normally be prudent to hold a meaningful allocation in non-volatile investments. Given the risky and volatile nature of a portfolio heavily committed to shares it may be advisable to hold the balance in short-dated, quality, fixed-interest paper. This avoids the chance of simultaneous falls in equity and bond markets as happened in 1994. Heavy commitment to equities is sufficiently risky in itself without the added adventure of a long-duration bond portfolio!

At this stage we are considering asset allocation as long-term percentages based on acquiring investments at 'average' prices and achieving 'average' returns. One way of approaching this problem is to suggest that at least half and probably 60% of assets should be directed towards the principal objective. This would suggest 60% in property, cash and foreign assets for investors' pursuing the first objective of beating inflation. Investing to maximise returns may require a strategic asset allocation of at least 60% in local and foreign shares.

A second approach is to start with a basic allocation of one-third each in cash, property and shares and then bias the proportions towards those categories of investments more suited to the individual objectives.

Juggling the figures around, these two approaches produce much the same answers and the 'standard' or 'strategic asset allocations' for these two objectives might be:

Strategic Asset Allocation

OBJECTIVE	BEATING INFLATION	MAXIMISING RETURN
Local ordinary shares	20%	50%
Property	30%	10%
Foreign shares	20%	20%
Cash/short-dated fixed interest	30%	20%

The next step is to decide on maximum allocations. If the objective is to maximise returns then investors would presumably be prepared to invest (say) up to 40% each in property and foreign stocks and up to 65% in local stocks with perhaps a minimum of 15% in cash and at the other extreme a maximum of 75% in cash.

In practice few superannuation trustees seeking to maximise returns on a long-term basis would approach these limits, particularly at the conservative end, because they will be keeping a close eye on the activities of fellow trustees elsewhere.

Much the same reasoning would apply to investors seeking, as their first priority, a return which exceeded inflation in the long term, except that such investors should be wary of an unexpected increase in the rate of inflation and may not be prepared to commit more than 40% to local shares and would probably wish to retain at least 20% in property.

Accordingly, the asset allocation *ranges* for investors with these objectives could be as follows:

Asset Allocation Ranges

LONG-TERM INVESTMENT OBJECTIVE	BEATING INFLATION		MAXIMISING RETURN	
Asset class	Min (%)	Max (%)	Min (%)	Max (%)
Local ordinary shares	0	40	25	65
Property	20	40	0	40
Foreign shares	5	30	0	40
Cash/short-dated fixed interest	25	75	15	75

Note that these two columns both add up to a figure in excess of 100%. These figures are limits, the actual proportion invested in the various sectors at any time — the actual asset allocation — must be less than these figures. In some instances these limits may be set by law. For example, under the former (1986) Victorian Friendly Societies Act, the allocation limits relating to ordinary shares, property and/or property trusts and foreign securities were 50%, 33% and nil respectively.

A second limit which needs to be determined is the maximum proportion of a portfolio which can be held in any one property or security. (It is usual to exempt bank or government-guaranteed assets from this requirement.) In this respect, one particular problem often occurs in Australia because the country's largest company, BHP, represents such a large proportion of the stock market capitalisation that a portfolio which is (say) 50% invested in ordinary shares and which is weighted roughly in accordance with the stock market index will frequently violate fixed limits on individual assets.

Consideration of the nature of diversification arises if it is decided to buy shares in investment companies or listed property trusts. Such assets contain a spread themselves and diversification may already be achieved by buying shares in an investment company rather than in a direct investment.

Perhaps the limit on individual assets should be something of the order of 4% of a total portfolio — including uninvested cash balances — with a slightly higher percentage permitted when the asset in question is a diversified investment company or diversified listed property trust. Private individuals could perhaps relax this restriction to two months' income if this permits a higher limit.

A further restriction which needs to be considered relates to individual industries. It is quite possible for changes in the nature of whole industries to affect all companies in the same industry. Consequently, there should be a limit to the proportion of a portfolio which is invested in any one industry. This should perhaps be something of the order of 15%.

The purpose of these restrictions is to limit the effect of a major disaster affecting an individual company or a whole industry. These limits should perhaps be reviewed periodically in the light of experience but they should never be reviewed when a purchase is contemplated. With any luck there will be occasions when a security rises substantially after purchase and limits become violated using latest market values even though the limits were not violated at the time of purchase. In these circumstances it might be wise to have a point at which partial sale is compulsory. For example, if the maximum purchase is 4% of the portfolio then half a holding should perhaps be immediately sold if the proportion were to rise to 6% — unless this would create severe tax complications.

While superannuation trustees will be required to document these decisions, it might not be a bad discipline for private investors to write them down too even though they are not binding.

In the case of the bottom-up approach, normally associated with value-oriented investing, asset allocation is a by-product of the selection of individual assets. The investor looks for the best bargains, decides what percentage to invest in each, and stops when any limits are reached. If insufficient opportunities can be found then the funds are left uninvested, at call or in short-dated government or bank guaranteed investments.

It follows therefore that the investor needs to decide whether the top-down or bottom-up approach will be adopted before considering the question of asset allocation. If a bottom-up approach is to be taken then asset allocation is a by-product of the selection of individual assets and any fixed limits.

If a top-down approach is to be used then it has to be decided who is going to make this decision, and those responsible for the decision will need to make it explicitly. For example, the trustees of a superannuation fund could purchase units in a specialised unit trust and delegate the asset allocation decision by this action. Alternatively, they could appoint a fund management organisation subject to specific instructions, subject to change on notice, and retain the asset allocation decision themselves. Another possible approach would be to purchase interests in a number of 'packaged' products which achieved the desired asset allocation outcome.

In other words, investors who choose a top-down approach need to make up their mind at the outset how far the 'asset allocation' decision is to be delegated. Investors who opt for the bottom-up approach need to monitor their investments against sector and asset class limits.

DEVIATIONS FROM STANDARD PORTFOLIO POLICY

The idea of holding an equity (or any other primary asset class) component which, as a matter of temporary implementation, deviates significantly from standard is called 'tactical asset allocation'.

At first glance it would seem sensible to deviate from a standard (or strategic) position whenever the likely return from one asset class was particularly attractive or unattractive. While this sounds simple and logical in theory, its practice quite often leads to perverse effects. For example, the time to increase an exposure to ordinary shares is quite often when the general opinion is quite the opposite, just as the time to quit ordinary shares altogether may be when the majority of people in the investment community think that such a policy would be idiotic.

In consequence, there is a significant risk that deviations from the standard portfolio structure will be made at the wrong time, if such changes are based on forecasts of likely price movements. Unless such variations are based on a fundamental evaluation of the sector as a whole, the genuine long-term investor might be better off with the standard asset allocation applied in a semi-automatic fashion. On the other hand, deviations based on value judgements — as distinct from forecasts — can lead to ill-informed criticism of trustees if these value judgements turn out to be opposite to market opinion in the short term. In this respect private investors, being responsible to no-one other than themselves, enjoy a distinct advantage over their 'performance oriented' professional counterparts.

As with the selection of individual securities, an evaluation of property and ordinary share asset classes can be based on a mixture of forecasts and value judgements. In the case of ordinary shares the three key value indicators are dividend yields, price/earnings ratios, and the relationship between capitalisation and shareholders' funds. In the case of listed property trusts, all income is distributed and consequently the principal value indicators are income yield and the relationship between capitalisation and unit-holders' funds.

Let us now attempt a value-based evaluation of two asset classes — listed property trusts and Australian ordinary shares. By way of comparison, the 1992 figures are shown alongside those of 1997 as well as a review of the inferences drawn from the 1992 figures which appeared in the previous edition of this book.

SECTOR EVALUATION — LISTED PROPERTY TRUSTS

Based on published figures and analysts' forecasts of distributions, we can produce a form of aggregate or consolidated statistics to assess the listed property trust sector as a whole.

Most of these statistics are self-explanatory, except perhaps for price/net-assets ratio which is the aggregate market value of all listed property trusts divided by the aggregate unit-holders' funds and 'prospective yield' which is the estimated aggregate distributions to unit-holders divided by the aggregate market capitalisation. The ASX indices are the Australian Stock Exchange Property Trust price and accumulation indices.

The table below shows selected figures as at 30 June 1997 and 1992:

	1997	1992
Unit-holders' funds ($ billion)	17.6	9.1
Price/net-assets ratio	1.12	0.82
Prospective yield (%)	7.5	8.7
ASX price index	1,244	1,012
ASX accumulation index	11,014	5,962
Consumer price index	120.2	107.3
Annual rate of inflation over previous two years (%)	1.7	2.3
Yield on cash management trusts (%)	4.9	5.7
10-year bond rate (%)	7.0	8.9

Extracting this information requires a little research and effort. However, this is a relatively simple task compared to the next step of assessing and interpreting the information.[16]

In 1992, property valuations had fallen substantially, approximately 20% of all office blocks were vacant Australia-wide and those tenants who had recently renewed leases had extracted a number of concessions from landlords by way of 'rent holidays' and moving-in expenses. Thus rents were expected to fall further as existing leases were renewed, although the effective level of rentals was well below what would be required to stimulate new developments.

In the 1990s, the concept of property 'valuation' caused a number of headaches. For the purposes of this discussion the valuation is really an estimation of its current market value. Interestingly, property valuers began to mention the concept of 'long-term investment value' as well as the normal valuation. While the 'long-term investment values' of the buildings may well have fallen, the declines in long-term investment value would not have been nearly as severe as the declines in quoted 'valuations'. In this respect an important piece of information which is difficult to obtain is the replacement cost of the buildings underlying these trusts.

In 1992, the buildings underlying these listed trusts were probably valued at a discount of around 20% on replacement cost, which suggests that the listed units were trading at a level which, in aggregate, represented two-thirds of replacement cost.

The property market was clearly depressed and some further reductions in rents and property valuations were anticipated, although the reductions to come were not expected to be as large as in the previous two years. In so far as office accommodation was concerned the supply of new space was falling off.

The 1992 edition of *BluePrint for Investment* summarised the situation as follows:

"In the circumstances it was not surprising that the sentiment towards investment property had turned negative. However the income was substantially higher than that which could be obtained on cash investments, with plenty of scope for growth when demand recovered. This improvement would come from reduced vacancies as well as increased rent levels. Against this longer term optimism the likely reduction in rents and capital values in the short term were real negative factors although they were reflected in market prices – partially at least.

This would suggest that a long-term investor should probably have been following at least a standard exposure to property. The negative sentiments towards property expressed in the [financial press] may have been an accurate indicator of short-term performance but in the context of long-term investment the case against property was probably overstated."

Considering the rate of inflation and short-term interest rates over the five years to 1997, a total return of 13.1% per annum — determined by comparing ASX accumulation indices — seems to have vindicated this view.

However, no small part of the result owes its origin to a market reassessment of the merits of listed property trusts — as demonstrated in the decline in prospective yield from 8.7% to 7.5% and an increase in the price/net-assets ratio from 0.8 to 1.1.

While the ASX Property Trust price index has risen 20%, the value of unit-holders' funds has almost doubled, which means that roughly half the underlying property has been bought since 1992. In consequence the discount on the replacement value of the underlying property has been eroded by the issue of new units in existing trusts and the listing of new ones.

From an income point of view, the prospective yield in 1997 looks attractive relative to both cash management trusts and long-term government bonds. If anything, the income relationship between property trusts and government bonds has moved in favour of listed property trusts over the intervening five years. However, the more optimistic price/net-assets ratio is a mildly cautionary signal suggesting that investors who like to make 'tactical asset allocation' decisions should hold no more than a 'strategic' exposure to this asset class.

THE QUALITY OF QUANTITATIVE INVESTMENT DATA

This evaluation of listed property trusts assumes, to some extent, that the audited figures on which the analysis is based are reliable and up to date. This is not always the case. For example, one of the reasons advanced for the discount between market prices and underlying asset values in 1992 was the expectation that many of the underlying properties would be revalued downwards and trust distributions would be cut as expiring leases were renegotiated at lower rentals.

Subsequent developments demonstrated some truth in this observation – but not to the extent justified by the discount. In consequence, investors need to be able to assess investment statistics and concepts such as prospective yields. Unfortunately, this is the easy part. More difficult is the assessment of the quality of the information on which they plan to base their decisions. For the vast majority of investors, reports prepared by experienced investment analysts employed by share broking firms will be of great assistance in forming this assessment. This holds even if their purchase and sale 'recommendations' may need to be treated with care – as discussed later.

In respect of ordinary shares, quality of data – particularly of profits – is both more important and more difficult to assess. Companies have their good and bad years. Consequently the long-term investor is particularly interested in an assessment of the level of profits and dividends which are sustainable in the long term.

SECTOR EVALUATION — AUSTRALIAN ORDINARY SHARES

To avoid the potential embarrassment of a public analysis of an individual company's financial statements, let us attempt an assessment of a company which does not exist — the ASX All Ordinaries index — but which still represents a typical Australian share portfolio. The table below shows selected figures as at 30 June 1997 and 1992:

	1997	1992
'Prospective' price/earnings ratio	17x	15x
Dividend yield (50 Leaders) (%)	3.5	3.7
Price/net-assets ratio	2.3	1.6
Annual rate of inflation over previous two years (%)	2.3	1.7
10-year bond rate (%)	7.0	8.9

The casual observer may note that with the decline in the 10-year bond rate, some reduction in the dividend yield and an increase in the price/earnings ratio would be justified. This is a reasonable comment until the asset factor is taken into account.

If a price/net-assets ratio is divided by the price/earnings ratio, the net result is the earnings/net-assets ratio — or, broadly speaking, the return on shareholders' funds or **profitability**. It is therefore possible to calculate the return on equity capital or profitability that is implicit in market valuations from these two pieces of information.

In 1992, the profitability implied by the stock market valuations of the time was therefore 10.5% per annum; the corresponding figure in 1997 was 13.5%.

Market valuations rely, partially at least, on earnings and price/earnings ratios. Earnings depend on profitability and there is probably a tendency for price/earnings ratios to be higher in periods of high profitability. There is therefore a 'double whammy' effect if corporate profitability fails to meet market expectations. Not only will earnings fail to reach expectations, the valuations of these reduced earnings will be based, by the market, on a lower multiplier.

An investor therefore needs to be able to estimate the level of profitability implicit in market valuations and to assess whether these levels of profitability are sustainable. If this assessment turns out to be realistic, the investor needs to be able to capitalise these sustainable profits using a realistic price/earnings ratio to obtain a reasonable valuation of an individual stock or the market as a whole. What then is a sustainable level of profitability?

The Reserve Bank once published an aggregate balance sheet of a large number of listed companies which contains some of this information but it is by no means complete. Between 1960 and 1980 the Reserve Bank All Industries Constant Group showed an average rate of earnings on shareholders' funds of 8.5%, excluding extraordinary items. The estimates shown in Chapter 8 are a little higher.

This would suggest that the prospective estimates on which the market was trading in 1992 were slightly above the historic norm. Based on historical precedents, one might expect a price/earnings ratio of around 12x in the context of short-term interest rates of around 6%, so a prospective price/earnings ratio of 15x seemed a little high in 1992.

The 1992 edition therefore expressed doubts about both the level of 'earnings' on which the 'professional market' was basing its decisions, and also the capitalisation of those earnings. With the benefit of hindsight, these reservations appear to have been unfounded; not only had the level of profitability implied by market valuations been exceeded, the basis of capitalisation of these earnings had increased — leading to a significant increase in the ASX All Ordinaries index.

In 1997 however, these valuations have been stretched on two fronts. The implied profitability had increased to around 13.5% per annum after tax while the long-term bond rate has declined to 7%; furthermore, the prospective price/earnings ratio of 17x was further removed from historical norms.

Were investors who purchased share portfolios equivalent to the All Ordinaries index in June 1992 gifted in their assessment that ensuing profitability would exceed market expectations — and that price/earnings ratios would also expand a little over the next five years? Or were they just lucky? Perhaps we should remember the humbling remark, generally attributed to J.K. Galbraith, "that financial genius is a rising market!"

In 1997, the situation was somewhat different than five years earlier — and a great deal more different than the small decline in dividend yield and the modest increase in price/earnings ratios would indicate. Consequently, those investors who like to make tactical allocation decisions may have found it desirable to reduce their allocation to ordinary shares below standard in mid-1997. This appears to have been quite contrary to the mood at the time.

It was perhaps not surprising that value-oriented investors and 'bottom-up' fund managers were having trouble, in mid-1997, finding stocks which met their value criteria. Also, there was the spectre of Wall Street valuations at the time. The table below compares stock market valuations in Australia, the United Kingdom and the United States of America in mid-1997.

Selected Market Indicators — June 1997

Country	USA	UK	Australia
Index	S&P 500	FTA All Share	ASX All Ords
Dividend yield (%)	1.8	2.5	3.5
Price/net-assets ratio	5.2	3.5	2.3
Prospective price/earnings ratio	25	20	17
Implicit profitability (%)	25	17	13

It is left to the reader to consider the analysis of this chapter in relation to these valuations, and to History to sit in judgement in due course!

Chapter 5

Investors' Interests, Corporate Governance and the Investment Industry

CORPORATE OBJECTIVES

THE INVESTMENT process inevitably involves the use of custodians — defined in a broad sense — such as superannuation fund trustees and company directors who are responsible for the organisations in which investors own shares. The investment process may also involve portfolio managers and intermediaries such as share brokers, real estate agents and investment consultants.

One might think at first that in a capitalist system the objective of all company directors and managers is to provide maximum returns to the shareholders who either elect or pay them. Consumers would be protected by competition between firms offering similar products which would restrict all firms to making a return on capital which is not excessive.

Alas, the world is not so simple. As far as corporate management and the financial services industry is concerned, the interests of investors, be they clients or shareholders, can easily become a means to

115

an end rather than an end in themselves. This is less true of superannuation fund trustees whose responsibilities are far more focused on beneficiaries.

Besides company directors and superannuation fund trustees, there is a variety of financial institutions, small businesses and other organisations operating in the investment industry. Like company management, service to investors can also be a means to an end rather than an end in itself. For their own benefit, investors need to understand the motivation of these organisations so that they can make allowance for any conflicts in their dealings with the industry.

Let us begin this discussion of relationships between investors and the investment world by considering the corporate management of listed companies. Company directors have numerous pressures to deal with such as those emanating from political parties, government agencies, litigants, senior management and other personnel, industry bodies, journalists, trade unions, charities and environmentalists. Shareholders' interests are therefore only one of a number of considerations for directors and managers to consider in their deliberations and decisions. Some would argue that many companies give insufficient weight to their shareholders' interests, and the ability of shareholders to 'vote with their feet' by selling their shares may lessen this pressure.

A clue to corporate behaviour, as far as shareholders are concerned, is contained in some observations as to when they become important. Shareholders suddenly become very important when a company is under threat of takeover. To quote Alan Geddes, formerly managing director of Mercantile Mutual Life writing in 1974:[1]

"Takeover bids are exciting for the shareholders in the company receiving the bid. The shareholders of the company making the bid are treated in the customary manner (i.e. not consulted unless an increase of capital is required for the purpose) but the shareholders of the quarry company suddenly become important for the first time, being wooed by their own directors and those of the assailant, and presented with facts and promises which otherwise would have remained beyond their imagination."

There was a touch of irony when Mercantile Mutual was itself subject to a takeover offer a couple of years later.

Robert Townsend in *Up the Organisation* wrote:[2]

"As is well known, the big corporation's priorities are:

1. *Care and feeding of the chief executive, his entourage, and the board of directors (mostly his friends, put there by him to ensure the tranquillity of his reign).*

2. *Management.*

3. *Employees.*

4. *Customers.*

5. *(Way down the line) Stockholders."*

To some extent these quotations are only anecdotal evidence, so readers will need to consider whether these observations correspond with their own. A more formal study of corporate objectives was conducted in 1970 by Patrick Rivett, subsequently Professor of Operational Research at the University of Sussex. Rivett conducted a survey of 300 organisations in the United Kingdom to ascertain their organisational objectives. He received 70 genuine replies of which he noted:[3]

"... within the replies from the private enterprise companies it was interesting to note that only two of the 30 organisations in this group has _any_ mention of the shareholders."

It must have been a difficult task to decipher such a variety of replies into neat categories but Rivett was able to conclude:

"...three main areas and topics were common to most of the replies... These three basic objectives of organisations emerged as:

(a) **Survival.** *... Sometimes within the private sector survival of the organisation is taken as being synonymous with survival of the senior management, particularly if a take-over battle is in prospect....*

(b) **Growth.** *Almost without exception, every organisation wanted to grow. ... (One has yet to meet a Vice-Chancellor who does not wish his university to increase in size.) ...*

(c) **Maximization of well-being.** *This is different from maximization of profitability and indeed only one organisation out of*

those who replied had maximisation of profitability as an objective. <u>It seems well understood that profitability is not an end but a means to an end</u>. Most managers, particularly in the higher echelon wish to enjoy what they are doing. Profitability at a level which enables them to deal with shareholders' needs, to ensure the survival of the organisation, means that from then on management can start to enjoy themselves.

This suggests that shareholders', directors' and managers' interests are closest when survival is at stake. When things are going well, there is a natural tendency for these interests to diverge and not necessarily with the interests of shareholders at the top of the list of priorities. Critics may argue that Rivett's survey was too long ago — but has human nature really changed that much in the last 30 years?

COMPANY TAKEOVERS

One circumstance in which the interests of proprietors and senior management can conflict is during a takeover. As Geddes suggested there are usually immediate benefits for the shareholders of the quarry at the expense (in the short term at least) of the shareholders of the aggressor.

From a board and management perspective, takeovers are interesting psychological studies because it is often the survival of the board and senior management of the quarry which is at stake, while the growth of the business of the aggressor is enhanced. It does not necessarily follow that business growth enhances the value of the shares of the aggressor, particularly if more shares are issued to pay for the takeover.

One of the interesting findings of the study by Fama and French[4] was the conclusion that company size was a significant factor in determining investment returns. This so-called 'small company effect' has puzzled academics who believe in efficient markets. Observers of corporate behaviour, particularly in relation to acquisitions, would recognise that at least part of this effect has its root cause in observable human behaviour as documented by Rivett.

First of all, the desire to survive in their jobs will concentrate the efforts of directors and managers of smaller companies towards giving shareholders' interests a higher priority than might be the case in a company which was sufficiently large to deter takeovers. Second, when takeovers do occur it is usually the larger company taking over the smaller, thereby resulting in a transfer of wealth from the reserves of the larger company to the shareholders of the smaller company.

A more favourable view of the benefits of corporate takeovers to shareholders of the offeror company is presented by N.E. Renton in his authoritative text on corporate governance.[5] According to Renton:

> *"In general, companies launch takeover offers because they expect that increased profitability and other benefits will flow from such a move."*

He then lists the numerous benefits to shareholders of the offeror company which could flow from a takeover. However, Renton concedes:[6]

> *"... legislation does nothing to protect the interests of the shareholders in the offeror corporation. Yet these suffer if the terms of the offer are too generous."*

Whether companies launch takeovers for the benefits which will flow to their shareholders, or to satisfy the 'growth' objectives of the senior management and directors of the offeror, is a question which needs to be considered on a case-by-case basis. In general, however, the documented existence of the 'small company effect' suggests that, if takeovers are one reason for this phenomenon, then takeover offers have tended to be too favourable to offerees in the past.

Interestingly, Renton also feels that offeror companies should seek approval of their own shareholders before making a takeover offer in some circumstances:[7]

> *"If the takeover is going to increase the size of the assets and/or the number of shares on issue by more than, say, 10 per cent then ... consideration should be given to allowing the existing shareholders to have a vote on the matter in general meeting."*

DIVIDEND REINVESTMENT PLANS AND RIGHTS (CONSCRIPTION?) ISSUES

In many ways the existence of dividend reinvestment plans also illustrates this conflict between corporate growth and maximising investors' returns. Participants in dividend reinvestment plans are usually able to acquire, at a discount on the prevailing market price, additional shares in a company by assigning dividends back to the company for this purpose.

From the point of view of the company, dividend reinvestment plans can be a convenient source of equity capital and from the point of view of participants it is a cheap way of increasing their interest in the company. Unfortunately, there is some downside for those who do not participate in the plan for two reasons:

(a) The continued issue of shares at a discount dilutes their interest in the company

(b) The availability of cheap shares when dividends are paid may reduce the demand for the company's shares and in consequence the price may be permanently lower than it would be if the plan did not exist.

For those who participate in dividend reinvestment plans there is perhaps a short-term advantage in acquiring shares at a discount. But 'money does not grow on trees' and this advantage accrues at the expense of someone else — in this case those shareholders who do not participate. When shareholders who participate in dividend reinvestment plans eventually need to sell or terminate their participation, the disadvantages applying to non-participants will then apply to them.

In the meantime the record-keeping required for capital gains tax could easily outweigh the advantages of the plan discount.

Although this is difficult to quantify, a number of companies seem to have realised that dividend reinvestment plans dilute their performance as measured in growth of earnings per share. As a result there seems to be a developing trend towards suspension of these plans or at least reducing the discount at which such dividend reinvestment plan shares are offered.

A variation on the same theme is often presented when companies decide to raise additional shares from existing shareholders for expansion. The desire for expansion can sometimes compromise the interests of shareholders.

Rights issues are normally offered below the current ruling price, thereby ensuring that the 'rights' have some value. However, those shareholders who do not wish to take up their entitlement or who cannot afford to subscribe additional capital are faced with a double penalty. First, the rights issue immediately weakens the market in the company's shares, thereby reducing the value of their entitlement; second, the proceeds from rights sales are often subject to capital gains tax.

Perhaps some of these issues would be more appropriately called 'conscription' issues instead of 'rights' issues! In any event, it would be easy to make a case for protecting shareholders' interests by requiring an authorising resolution prior to such issues proceeding. Here is an example which occurred in March 1997:[8]

> *"Santos Ltd has been forced to seek its first capital raising in seven years after exercising its pre-emptive right to acquire WMC Ltd's East Spar oil and gas interests for $181 million ...*

> *"... Santos stock yesterday fell 14¢ ... and the company conceded that the issue would be 'modestly dilutive' to its earnings per share outlook."*

INVESTMENT ADVISERS — COMMISSION OR FEE-BASED ADVICE?

Following the collapse of the Poseidon boom, company laws were strengthened to prevent a recurrence of some of the excesses of this period. Also state-based legislation to regulate the securities industry was introduced in 1975. This legislation was eventually incorporated into the Federal Corporations Law in 1989.

With minor exceptions no-one is allowed to give investment advice or deal in 'securities' (a term which includes managed funds and unlisted property trusts as well as shares listed on the Australian Stock Exchange) unless they hold an appropriate licence or a 'proper authority' from a licensed organisation.

The legislation distinguishes between organisations which are merely allowed to act as advisers and dealers. Interestingly 'dealers' are allowed to both deal and advise but advisers are not allowed to deal. An essential commercial difference between a dealer and an adviser is whether their fees contain a commission element or not.

A booklet published jointly by the Australian Securities Commission and Financial Planning Association of Australia Limited in 1992, claimed (with qualification) that this regime contained some quality controls.[9]

> *"A licence to advise on securities is not a guarantee of good advice, but it means the ASC has screened the licensee for education and experience before granting the licence."*

Three years after the publication of this booklet the Australian Securities Commission embarked on a program intended to substantially increase the quality of investment advice.[10]

"The purpose of the Licensing Review is to improve the quality of advice securities advisers provide to investors."

This continued development may improve the quality controls enforced at entry, but the apparent need for continual change suggests that regulation will never suffice. The story is always the same — the existing legislation is inadequate and more rules and regulations are required. Perhaps this is further evidence of the desire for 'growth' documented by Rivett; having achieved its influence in the industry, the Australian Securities Commission will continue to seek greater rather than less control over the industry — and any problems will be used as a pretext for increasing its control.

Perhaps an ASC licence may indicate a preparedness to comply with the law, but it would be foolhardy for an investor to rely on ASC screening for education and experience.

Consider for example, the educational requirement. As we saw in Chapter 1, successful investors can pursue a variety of academic interests, quite often unrelated to the investment world, before commencing an investment career. Conversely, there could be considerable dangers in accepting the educational qualifications of people who have devoted their undergraduate years to a study of efficient market theory. So there can be no hard and fast rules as to what is an appropriate educational requirement which makes the value of this screening process difficult to assess.

Now consider the experience requirement. There is a considerable difference between a licensee who has had 10 years experience as an investment analyst and someone who has spent the same amount of time selling packaged investment products. This makes the experience requirement equally difficult to evaluate. In this respect it is interesting to note that the Financial Planning Association permits its members to accrue 'continuing professional development' points by attending seminars on business skills as well as those directly related to improving the quality of their advice.

This emphasis on education, experience and training is directed at improving the competence of 'investment advisers'. From the point of view of the investing public, investors may think that this search for regulated 'competence' is concerned with competent advice and this seems to be the intention as expressed by the chairman of the Australian Securities Commission before a parliamentary committee:[11]

"... [investment advisers are licensed because] the clients of investment advisers simply are not in a position to judge for themselves the competence and the qualifications of the people who hold themselves out as investment advisers."

Unfortunately the public, who interpret competence as implying an ability to provide competent advice, are the unwitting subject of a legislative hoax. How can an organisation which is not itself recognised as competent to provide investment advice, and which has no experience in doing so, judge the competence of others to provide competent advice? It is not surprising, therefore, that the Australian Securities Commission, which is responsible for this regulation invented a new meaning for the word competence in its administration of advisers. It sees 'competence' as a compliance issue:[12]

"... our assessment of competence is more about whether people understand the need to disclose their conflicts and the need to ensure that they have understood what their clients want. It is obviously not about the ultimate performance of investment advisers."

If this approach were adopted in the aviation industry — another example of government licensing — a competent pilot would be someone who knew how to keep a log book neatly and who knew to check the destination before departure. Testing a pilot's ability to fly an aeroplane with safety would be left to passengers!

To put this another way, if the Australian Securities Commission's approach to competence were used in the aviation industry much of the testing of pilots would be posthumous. It is perhaps not surprising therefore, that the poor quality of some advice in the securities industry is also detected posthumously — after investors have lost their money.

This is intended as a criticism of the philosophy behind the legislation rather than a criticism of the Australian Securities Commission which is charged with administering counterproductive aspects of the Corporations Law. For some reason, the public, the

Commission and politicians seem to place great faith in a legislative and/or regulatory solution to the quality of investment advice.

The impracticality of any official certification of advisory competence — as the term would be interpreted by the investing public — and the misconceptions of competency created by the existence of licences leaves the average investor highly susceptible to skilled advertising and salesmanship. There is always the danger that the public will tend to 'judge the book by its cover'. As Austin Donnelly puts it:[13]

"Successful marketing has achieved prominence in the investment advisory field for many people who were in completely different occupations ten years ago and for others whose experience is entirely in marketing investment products, rather than objectively assessing the plus and minus factors for various investments."

A further problem for novices dealing with investment advisers is the fact that consultants providing impartial fee-based advice and representatives of organisations which derive most of their income from commission are often both known as 'investment advisers'. Even if representatives of 'licensed dealers' are salaried employees, their salaries, bonuses and/or jobs would usually be dependent on the commissions generated by the business they place.

There has been much debate in the investment advisory industry as to whether commission or fees is the most appropriate form of remuneration. The potential conflict inherent in commission-based advice is clear. It is perhaps unfortunate, therefore, that because dealers can both 'deal' and 'advise' whereas advisers can only 'advise', the adviser's licence is seen in the industry as junior to the dealer's licence. As a result of this semi-official ranking, the relative value of fee-based advice may have been inadvertently undermined.

It is interesting to note that one organisation, established to represent the interests of the consumers in the investment industry, claimed in a submission to a government enquiry that:

"we have had no complaints against advisers operating on a fees only basis."[14]

The same organisation complained that they had terminated their list of advisers operating on a fees-only basis partly because the list had become so short.

With the introduction of 'no load' products and 'rebateable commissions' there has emerged a trend towards fee-based advice in the last few years and investors can make up their own mind as to which they prefer. However, human nature being what it is, investors who genuinely need fee-based advice will still expect high quality 'advice' for nothing and blame everyone but themselves when they lose money.

STOCKBROKERS

Prior to the introduction of laws licensing dealers and investment advisers, seeking investment advice generally meant a visit to the person's normal stockbroker. Someone seeking advice for the first time usually asked around and arranged an introduction. The existence of this traditional arrangement by which brokers both 'deal' and 'advise' was recognised by laws requiring broking companies or members of broking partnerships to hold dealers' licences. In addition, stockbrokers are subject to other requirements which the stock exchange places on its members.

These firms derive most of their income from commissions on transactions they undertake on behalf of their 'clients', however some firms with specialised interests such as underwriting may derive significant amounts of income in other ways. It would be unusual for a share broker to charge a flat fee for an interview.

Broking organisations employ a variety of people to conduct their business of which the most important from their customers' point of view are the client 'advisers'.

Client advisers deal directly with clients most of the time, taking instructions, answering questions, offering suggestions and liaising between the client and other departments of the firm. To some extent customers tend to drift towards the adviser with whom they feel most comfortable. The 'young guns' tend to deal with financial institutions because institutional business tends to be placed by 'young guns' at the other end of the telephone.

Private individuals, however, may prefer to deal with more experienced people who, with time, develop a good understanding of their clients' requirements in addition to general market experience and knowledge acquired over many years — if not decades. The lessons learned in 1987 and 1974 will not have been forgotten by those who experienced them. Investors with shorter memories may therefore derive considerable benefit from dealing with an adviser whose experience covers 1987 – at least.

Behind the 'client advisers', the next most important group of people for the average investor are the research analysts. They study company balance sheets, earnings reports, trade magazines and other relevant economic data and routinely brief broking firms' client advisers and prepare written reports.

Broking analysts' research reports are a valuable source of information for investors, so it is important to gain an appreciation of their value and recognise their limitations. Of particular importance is the fact that reports on individual companies usually contain a 'recommendation'. In institutional circles these recommendations are often treated with a great deal of cynicism (although it is quite likely that they have some psychological effect), and academic studies have tended to support the view that such 'recommendations' should not be taken seriously.[15]

Notwithstanding these reservations about analysts' recommendations it would be wrong to conclude that broking research reports have little value. Reports on individual stocks are usually thorough and prepared by experienced, well-trained industry specialists who have a great deal of pride in their work. Experienced analysts are far more likely to spot 'creative accounting' and unsustainable profitability than the lay investor. Furthermore, security analysts quickly develop a reputation for the quality of their work in a small world. A top-flight analyst is a highly marketable commodity and as a result there are significant incentives for quality in the ranks of security analysts.

As a result, analysts' reports generally provide a great deal of useful and accurate factual information on individual companies, as well as less reliable 'estimates' and 'recommendations'. The discerning reader will therefore find real value in research reports if the 'estimates' are critically evaluated and the 'recommendations' are treated with caution.

Most of the analysts' work, particularly in the larger firms, is oriented towards generating business from financial institutions, but it is often available on request to smaller private investors. This may not be quite so generously available in the future as firms are discovering that smaller clients are using their research, but then placing their business elsewhere with a 'discount' broker providing 'execution only' cut-price services.

RESEARCH OF UNLISTED INVESTMENTS

An important development in the investment industry in the last 10 years is the growth of organisations which conduct research into packaged financial products and sell the information to advisers. The growth of these research houses has been partially stimulated by legislation which requires advisers to have a 'reasonable basis' on which to make any 'recommendation'.[16]

In the case of sharebrokers, this research material comes from their own analyses, but 'advisers' without their own research facilities, such as the smaller operators who deal mainly in packaged products, are effectively forced to obtain research material from third parties.

The number of packaged financial products on offer is considerable. From this universe, the research houses regularly publish a recommended list of products for their subscribers. However, the sheer number of products on issue inevitably results in much of the research outside the 'recommended list' being superficial.

Organisations offering investment 'advice' are required to ensure that their representatives are properly supervised in their advising role. One way in which this requirement is often met, in practice, is to require 'advisers' (i.e. 'proper authority' holders from a licensed organisation) to adhere closely to a recommended list.

In consequence, the net effect of these two legislative requirements is to vest considerable power over the destiny of large amounts of peoples' savings in the hands of research houses. This was probably not intended by either the regulators or the research houses, but it has become a fact of life. In a letter to the editor of *Money Management* one 'adviser' complained:[17]

> *"As an investment adviser, if I am to maintain ASC compliance for the portfolios I present, **I am at the mercy of a research house for its recommendations**."*

There are many problems with this system. If the basis of the contract between the research house and the 'adviser' is a share of commission — albeit indirectly, then the research organisation could have a conflict of interest, which may possibly influence the composition of a recommended list. (There is no commercial sense in recommending a list of products which do not pay commission to a list of subscribers who are primarily commission based.)

As we have already seen, the influence of a research house can be widespread. This influence extends to organisations who do not conduct their own research and consequently are handicapped in their ability to assess the research they receive. This concentration of influence is probably far greater in the market for unlisted investments than it is with listed securities.

This concentrated influence of research houses is a potential source of instability — particularly when the underlying assets of a previously recommended product are not readily saleable. For example, when a research house recommends redemption of unlisted property trusts or mortgage trusts which had previously been recommended, this could cause difficulties if a large number of investors decided to act on the recommendation at once.

The available research is a mixture of qualitative analysis and performance measurement. Judging by material published in newspapers and magazines, the analysis of performance seems to be quite important. Given the sheer number of indirect investment products on the market, it would be surprising if many investment advisers have enough time to do much more than study the performance figures — which is a superficial form of research.

As research into unlisted products is a recent development it has not been subject to the same sort of historical analysis as sharebrokers' recommendations. However, the history of broking research would suggest that research houses' recommendations should also be treated with caution. When recommendations are based on performance data there seems to be little effective acknowledgement that performance figures generally lack statistical significance and therefore have little predictive value.

One wonders also how much recommendations depend on the size of a fund manager's business, prestige, investment fashion and marketing muscle. An article which appeared in *Personal Investment* commented:[18]

> "*Strong products are usually available from solid, high profile managers. The products they launch fit the needs of investors and their advisers, are managed in a true-to-label fashion, and show very good initial performance and support from investors. They then receive recognition from researchers and this leads to further increases in inflow of funds into these products ...*"

The adviser who claimed to be *"at the mercy of a research house"*, was quite critical of research houses' attitude to *"boutique"* organisations after some of their previous mistakes:[19]

"I cannot help wondering if after some of the problems of the property managers and Estate Mortgage (which they recommended) we are not seeing a case of boutique bashing with research houses simply hiding behind the perceived safety of larger fund managers."

Provided organisations who publish research into packaged products do not make any mistakes, this concentration of influence would be of no concern. But if they were to make a large and serious mistake the effect on the savings of a large section of the community could be quite significant. Past history does not provide any confidence that serious research errors will be avoided in future and community financial disasters, such as the unlisted property trust debacle around 1990, will not recur. Is this not yet another example of unfortunate consequences following from well-meaning legislation?

FUND MANAGERS AND PERFORMANCE

Investors who choose to invest indirectly by way of managed funds, rollover funds and/or equity trusts have, by this choice, delegated the task of buying and selling individual investments to another organisation. Some years ago, the term 'financial institution' was used within the industry to refer to organisations such as portfolio management organisations, life offices, trustee companies, pension funds operating their own investments, foreign investment trusts and so on.

However, the legal distinctions between different types of organisations responsible for making buy and sell decisions has become increasingly blurred and the term 'fund manager' is commonly used to describe these organisations as well as the individual fund managers they employ.

Once a reasonable level of business has been achieved, fund management organisations are highly profitable. Survival and an adequate level of profitability are then assured. This leaves senior management free to concentrate on the main 'game' — growth of funds under management — by which success is usually measured.

From the clients' or investors' point of view, what really matters is the return on their money or 'performance'. 'Investment performance' is also important for fund managers because it attracts publicity, generates interest from prospective clients — possibly dissatisfied with their performance elsewhere — and keeps the existing clientele contented. Good performance retains existing business and helps attract new business on which profitability depends.

Where investors do not deal directly with a fund manager, advisers find it very much easier to 'recommend' a fund manager who has 'performed' over one which has not, even if they would do the opposite with their own money.

In the case of organisations such as life insurance companies, senior management will take a great deal of interest in the activities of the investment department because the growth of the organisation depends, to a considerable extent, on its performance. Similar comments would apply to the fund management activities of banks and trustee companies.

It has become rare for large superannuation funds to handle their own investments. As a result, superannuation trustees are vitally interested in the activities of the fund managers to whom they have delegated this task. In the case of accumulation funds, the benefits of members will depend on investment results, while in the case of defined benefit plans the cost to the employer will depend on investment results. In either case, there will be pressure to seek performance.

Given investors' desire for performance, it is not surprising that fund management organisations are oriented, in theory, towards achieving it. Senior employees attend economic briefings, strategy meetings and study all sorts of material — including brokers' research reports. While performance may not itself be the corporate objective of fund managers, their real objective — growth of funds under management — depends on it. So where is conflict of interest, if any, between fund managers and their clients, given their common interest in performance?

The answer to this question lies not in positive performance but in the different effect of losses on the two groups. By long experience, fund managers have learned that what really matters is relative performance — mildly poor results are grudgingly accepted by clients provided other managers produce similarly poor results. On the other hand missing out on a major stock market advance will not be tolerated.

When all managers hold similar positions and markets go down clients lose money and managers retain their business. If markets go up and managers are underweight then clients should still have reasonable results, but they will not be as good as other investors and the fund manager will risk losing the business.

What happens when a market is grossly overpriced? Advocates of efficient market theory would argue that this is a rare event but history suggests otherwise. Fund managers cannot afford the **business risk** of being substantially underweight in grossly overpriced markets in case a grossly overpriced market becomes even more grossly overpriced.

In the cold hard light of day, investors in general, and superannuation trustees in particular, would rarely admit to speculation. However, who is responsible if the widespread desire for performance leads to widespread speculation by creating a **business risk** for fund managers who do not speculate with their clients' funds in overpriced markets?

In the last 10 years there has been increasing use of 'benchmarks' or published portfolio structure in broad asset classes by fund managers offering collective investments for public subscription. Fund managers can therefore argue that by retaining overpriced assets they are merely adhering to their published benchmarks and satisfying investors' requirements — no matter how ill-conceived.

Even if they choose to delegate the day-to-day decisions to professionals via managed funds or individually-managed portfolios, investors still need to be able to relate investment markets to their own requirements.

Chapter 6

Packaged Financial Products and Indirect Investment

DIRECT VERSUS INDIRECT INVESTMENT

THERE ARE a number of points which need to be raised on the issue of direct versus indirect investment. In this context, direct investment refers to the purchase of shares in listed companies, individual properties, government bonds and bank accepted bills of exchange. Indirect investment refers to such investments as units in equity trusts, listed property trusts, cash management trusts and 'managed' funds.

Direct investment gives the investor more control, particularly in relation to the purchase and sale of individual assets. However, the paperwork associated with an investment of $1,000 is much the same as that associated with $10,000. This has led to minimum fixed components in most transaction fees — typically $50 to $100 per security.

On the basis of acquisition costs, indirect investment is therefore cheaper than direct investment for smaller amounts. On the other hand, indirect investment usually involves ongoing administration and/or management fees and there will be a point above which direct investment in the same underlying assets becomes more cost-effective.

By way of example, consider a portfolio of (say) 10 securities with equal amounts in each compared with an equity trust. Individual direct transaction costs might be 2% with a minimum of $75 per security. The equity trust might have an initial fee of 5% and ongoing management expenses of 1.5% per annum. In these circumstances the initial and ongoing costs of direct and indirect investment would be:

AMOUNT INVESTED	$10,000	$20,000	$50,000
Equity trust expenses			
Initial	$500	$1,000	$2,500
Ongoing	$150	$300	$ 750
Direct portfolio costs			
Initial	$750	$750	$1,000

Investors often use packaged products for convenience. For example investors with substantial portfolios may decide to invest the cash component in a pool which specialises in money market instruments — such as a cash management trust — rather than operating more directly for the sake of convenience. Private individuals can do this if they feel so inclined even if there is a cost disadvantage in how they operate, but superannuation fund trustees are more accountable for unnecessary costs and would need to consider the cost more carefully.

In the case of property, the vast majority of investors (by number) will be forced to invest indirectly to achieve reasonable diversity. In the case of shares, most serious investors should find that the logistics of direct investment do not represent any serious difficulty.

Finally, there are packaged products with special tax rules, such as superannuation pools and 'insurance bonds'. In these cases it may be impracticable for a private investor to operate directly. It is possible to run a one-person superannuation fund but the compliance costs are high; it may be preferable to operate indirectly until the size of the fund makes the additional expenses reasonable.

One aspect of indirect investment, which may require more attention in future, is the way in which an investment vehicle provides for tax on unrealised capital gains and the effect this may have on investors. For example, suppose an investor buys into a trust at $1.50 per unit and this price includes unrealised gains of (say) 50 cents. Let us now suppose that, as a result of redemptions, these gains need to be realised. In some circumstances these gains may need to be distributed and this may be subject to tax in the hands of the investor. Thus an investment with an apparent asset value of $1.50 per unit is suddenly transformed into an investment worth $1 per unit, a distribution of 50 cents per unit — less the tax liability attaching to this distribution.

This example may be a little extreme, but it illustrates the dangers of investing in investment pools without investigating any unrealised capital gains and the possible effect on the investor if such gains are realised.

CLOSED-END FUNDS AND OPEN-ENDED FUNDS

There are two distinct types of investment product classified by the way in which the investment pool expands and contracts. As the name implies closed-end funds have a fixed number of units or shares on issue. Subject to legal requirements, closed-end funds expand by issuing new units. This is usually done by an entitlement issue to existing unit-holders — new units are not continually on sale.

Unit-holders or shareholders of closed-end funds cannot redeem their investment. It is usual for closed-end funds to be listed and consequently unit-holders sell their interest on the open market.

In the case of open-ended funds new units are issued, and old units are redeemed at a price based on the market value of the underlying assets. With this facility for the issue and redemption of units, listing is not necessary.

To some extent the choice of open or closed-end fund is decided by the nature of the underlying investment. Where the underlying assets are actively traded and highly liquid, there should be no difficulty in expanding and contracting the investment pool at an accurately determined market value. An example of this is the cash management trust. It is theoretically possible for a cash management trust to be listed, however investors are usually investing in this sort of trust as an alternative to placing funds on deposit and the price fluctuations associated with listing would be unacceptable.

Where the investments are illiquid or where the market value is difficult to determine with any accuracy, a fund which is open-ended can get into trouble — for example the unlisted property trust market in

1990. The reason for this difficulty is twofold. First, the liquidity offered to investors is only partially backed by liquid assets. Second, a difficulty arises if the market value turns out to be inaccurate.

Consider, for example, the case of a property trust with 100 million units on issue with $50 million in cash and $50 million in property. Let us now suppose that half the unit-holders redeem their units at $1 and the property is then put on the market to restore some liquidity in the trust. Let us now suppose that the property valued at $50 million only turns out to be worth $30 million. Then, after the sale, the remaining 50 million units will only be backed by $30 million in cash. The value behind their investment will have fallen by 40% even though the total value of the trust as it stood before any redemptions will have only fallen 20% from $100 million to $80 million.

It seems somewhat unfair that, in this example, the unit-holders who precipitated what may have been a forced sale received in excess of the real market value of the assets underlying their units at the expense of those who remain. Investors can protect themselves against this by using closed-end funds (in this case listed trusts) so that if some of their fellow unit-holders wish to sell their investments at a time when the market for the underlying investment is depressed they are obliged to accept the going market price and the underlying assets are not disturbed.

In this respect one needs to be wary of the danger of potential recommendations of advisers if for some reason the product loses favour. They may become trigger-happy as a means of protecting their reputations. To quote an article in *Personal Investment:*[1]

> *"One observation..about trends in the industry is that advisers are now more likely to recommend redemption or switching out of a fund.*
>
> *"Advisers have learned an enormous amount over the last 10 years. ....*
> *Advisers have also become quite conscious of the last-man-out risk."*

In the case of an investment pool based on actively-traded securities such as the 'top 50' ordinary shares, there is no reason why investment 'vehicles' cannot be either closed-end or open-ended. The open-ended equity trust is usually sold by prospectus net of an 'up-front' of around 5%, and redeemed at net asset value. Whereas the closed-end fund, perhaps better known as an investment company, is usually traded on the stock exchange. The question as to whether an investor should subscribe for units in an equity trust (an open-ended pool) or buy shares in an investment company (a closed-end pool) needs to be analysed according to the circumstances at the time.

Some equity pools, such as those restricted to small companies and unlisted ones, would be better operated on a closed-end basis because of the limited marketability of the underlying assets.

Thus an investor investing indirectly will be safer using closed-end pools, such as listed property trusts and investment companies when the underlying assets suffer from limited marketability. This does expose investors to price volatility but it will protect the value of the underlying assets if fellow investors decide they wish to sell at a time when the market for the underlying assets is depressed. These general observations are particularly important where property is involved.

PROPERTY INVESTMENT POOLS

Once investors of modest or moderate means have accepted (perhaps reluctantly) that direct property investment is not ideal, the focus turns to indirect ways of achieving a beneficial interest in property. In pursuit of this objective it must be borne in mind that the purpose is to seek an alternative to property ownership. Property development is a distinctly different activity and not considered here.

There are four basic structures (or vehicles to use merchant bankers' jargon) to achieve beneficial property ownership — listed trusts, unlisted trusts, life office pools, and private partnerships or syndicates. In some countries there may also be listed companies whose business is property ownership rather than development but this is unusual in Australia.

It goes without saying that the property portfolio itself will determine to a large extent how the beneficial owners fare. This consideration will affect all properties no matter what the legal structure. In addition there are a number of important distinctions between these various structures.

For the purpose of this discussion the term 'unlisted trusts' refers to major trusts promoted to the public at large. The term does not refer to structures promoted privately or restrictively, which may be public unlisted trusts for the purposes of the Corporations Law, but which are syndicates, partnerships or private trusts in layman's language.

Perhaps the most important difference between various property pool structures is the method by which new investors become beneficial owners and the exit route for departing beneficiaries. In the case of listed trusts, the units are simply traded on the open market. This creates a problem in that the market price may not always reflect fair value for the underlying property and therefore a departing beneficiary may not receive fair value for sale on an investment to the direct benefit of the new investor.

In theory, unlisted trusts solve this problem by issuing and redeeming units at net asset value. Unfortunately, this proved to be impossible in the early 1990s when a severe national economic downturn prompted many unit-holders to seek to redeem their investment at a time when the property market was itself recessed and unable to absorb property already on the market for sale, let alone the additional sales required to redeem investments in unlisted trusts.

Reflecting on the events of the early 1990s it was perhaps unfair that those who 'got in first' received redemption values which were based on property valuations which turned out to be too high, and as a result the remaining investors had to bear the effect of generosity to early departees as well as the subsequent asset write-downs.

Ongoing unit-holders in unlisted trusts can also be disenfranchised when new units are issued shortly before a significant (upwards) property revaluation. The prospect of an impending revaluation could be used verbally to assist in the sale of new units.

In theory, the trustee of listed and unlisted trusts should have enough powers to ensure that unit-holders are treated fairly. In reality, however, the art and practice of property valuation is not always as accurate and timely as it needs to be for the purpose of enabling trustees to fulfil any moral obligation to see that ongoing unit-holders do not suffer at the expense of incoming or departing unit-holders.

A second problem with unlisted trusts is that a fair degree of liquidity is required to facilitate redemption. As a result, $100 invested in an unlisted trust may be represented by only $70 in property and $30 in cash which prevents the desired level of property investment being achieved without over-investment — that is to say $140 may need to be invested in an unlisted trust in normal times to ensure an underlying investment of $100 in property.

For these two reasons — achieving a full 100% investment in property for the investor's outlay and reducing the unpredictable effects of incoming and departing investors – the genuine long-term, indirect, property investor would be advised to stick with listed rather than unlisted trusts.

CAN NOVICE INVESTORS COMPETENTLY DELEGATE?

Many investors invest indirectly in equity trusts and 'managed' funds because they do not feel confident in selecting an individual share portfolio for themselves, or because they are nervous about making their own 'asset allocation' decisions.

There is an intuitive logic to the idea that non-experts should leave it to the experts. However, the decision to delegate for knowledge reasons raises the important question as to whether the delegator possesses sufficient knowledge to make an appropriate delegation decision. Investors, therefore, need to address the serious philosophical question as to whether those who do not feel confident of selecting their own portfolio are qualified to monitor the activities of the management of the indirect investments they have chosen.

In the really big league, the multi-million or billion dollar superannuation funds, it is quite common to appoint external managers for part or all of the investments of a fund. Trustees are therefore faced with a decision as to whom to delegate this responsibility, for which they often rely on independent advice. This raises the consideration as to the qualifications and experience required of independent investment consultants who offer such advice.

A person who aspires to the supervision of professional people in (say) law, medicine, accountancy or the armed services would normally progress from academic study through practical experience to a supervisory position. Thus, an analysis of the way people are promoted to supervisory positions in professionally-staffed organisations as diverse as hospitals, the armed services and life offices would suggest that it would be unusual to assume a supervisory position or consultancy without first understanding, at first hand, the activities of middle management and junior personnel.

If the world of the investment consultant was like many other professions, one might expect the novice to complete some form of relevant tertiary training and then start out analysing financial statements under the supervision of a more experienced colleague. The next step would be formulating judgements on individual securities, followed by making decisions on these judgements — which is the recognised position of portfolio manager. Finally, the experienced portfolio manager might be promoted to the more senior position of supervising portfolio managers.

For some reason or other the investment advisory industry does not work this way. People who have little or no first-hand experience of investment analysis or portfolio management offer their services to investors on the selection of 'managed' funds or, in the big league, the appointment of portfolio managers. There must be some doubt as to whether investors or trustees should rely on strategic advice from consultants whose experience of investment has been earned observing rather than participating in investment markets.

When an investor decides to buy a packaged product on the basis of advice, the nature of the experience of the person offering the advice is most important. There is a world of difference between experience gained analysing corporate financial statements and/or making investment decisions and experience gained 'marketing' packaged products. In the 'advising' industry it was quite common for a dealer's licence to permit the licensee to offer 'advice' on packaged products but not individual listed securities. This suggests that the Australian Securities Commission may also have thought that providing 'advice' on packaged products is easier than advising on individual securities.

If the packaged products are conventional and conservative it may be adequate to provide advice on these products in general terms, without a great depth of understanding of the underlying assets, in much the same way as it might be possible to bet on the jockeys at the race track if it is known that the horses are much the same. However, a great deal of money was lost in the crash of 1987 by selecting jockeys who liked riding wild horses which had got off to a good start.

An investor should therefore be wary of indirect investments and advice thereon unless the underlying assets are conventional and conservative. If the investment operations or the underlying assets are unusual in any way — of which unusually good short-term performance is often a symptom — then the investor needs to be able to base any decision on a clear understanding of the underlying nature of the product, and not pay much attention to performance figures. A 'recommendation' primarily based on 'superior performance' is likely to be both shallow and speculative.

This discussion carries a warning that investors who are not comfortable with direct investment — through lack of confidence in what they are doing — need to exercise some care to ensure that they are buying an appropriate investment product and not a speculative one. Somewhere along the line a thorough analysis should have been conducted.

Buying a packaged product does not relieve investors of responsibility for seeing that this has been done, even if they have not performed the analysis themselves. Drooling over 'investment performance' figures does not constitute a thorough analysis. An investor who is 'recommended' to buy a particular product should ask to see a more fundamental analysis of the product and an appraisal of the team responsible for investment decisions.

For the same reasons, trustees of large superannuation funds who use external investment management organisations should periodically seek an independent report on the investments of the portfolio as distinct from a report on its performance. 'Performance data' can easily disguise speculative activity which can only be investigated by looking at a full list of the actual stocks held, individual transactions and the reasons for them. There is anecdotal evidence to suggest that seeking an independent investment report as distinct from a performance report may be a novel idea.

WHAT IS A CONVENTIONAL SHARE PORTFOLIO?

As discussed, investors who are buying 'packaged products' because they do not feel confident of making their own decisions, need to exercise special care if the underlying investments are unconventional. This then leads to the question of a definition of a conventional portfolio.

It is very much easier to define a conventional portfolio negatively — to say what a conventional portfolio is not rather than what it is. For example, any of the following would indicate a portfolio which is not conventional:

(a) Large holdings in companies which are not household names.

(b) Concentration in a particular area — such as banks or media stocks.

(c) Anything more than a negligible use of derivative instruments such as futures and options contracts.

(d) Big changes in major individual holdings from year to year.

Quite a good way of quickly checking an investment portfolio is to list the 10 largest holdings in decreasing order of size and to compare this list with the market capitalisation of companies also shown in decreasing order published periodically in the press and specialist magazines. A more sophisticated approach is to compare the holding, as a percentage of the portfolio with the 'weightings' of the Australian All Ordinaries index.

For example, the following table compares index weightings and portfolio weightings of a listed investment company on two dates. The 1992 figures indicated a fairly conventional portfolio at the time:[2]

Portfolio Weightings Versus Index Weightings as at 30/6/92

COMPANY	PORTFOLIO WEIGHTING %	INDEX %
BHP	14.0	12.5
National Bank	6.6	5.2
News Corporation	5.0	4.3
CRA	4.6	4.5
BTR Nylex	4.3	3.6
Coles Myer	3.6	3.6
MIM Holdings	3.2	2.3
Western Mining	3.3	2.7
CSR	2.6	2.1
Pacific Dunlop	2.6	2.5
TOTAL	49.8	43.3

By way of contrast, the 1996 figures in the following table indicate a significant change of policy in the intervening four years.

Portfolio Weightings Versus Index Weightings as at 30/6/96

COMPANY	PORTFOLIO WEIGHTING %	INDEX %
BHP	20.1	10.9
News Corporation (all issues)	9.1	6.3
National Bank	7.8	5.4
WMC	6.3	3.2
Westpac	6.2	3.2
Pioneer International	4.7	1.0
ANZ	3.5	2.8
GIO	3.4	0.6
Qantas	3.2	0.7
Lend Lease	3.2	1.4
TOTAL	67.5	35.5

While the selection of a packaged product which is unconventional requires more than the usual caution, it does not follow that such a course should be avoided. In this case, the managers of the company seemed to be prepared to back their judgement and consequently investment results may not be typical of the market as a whole.

TAXATION, 'UP-FRONTS' AND 'ONGOINGS'

In the case of indirect investments a number of factors, besides investment results, affect the way in which the investor fares in the end. These matters are taxation (which becomes a factor when special rules apply), fees charged 'up-front' on packaged products (or charges involved in purchasing listed investments), and ongoing expenses. In this respect investors should not forget the time and effort involved in keeping records and preparing tax returns if the direct route is taken.

For example, an investor with $10,000 to invest will probably pay ongoing expenses of around $150 if the investment is made indirectly.

But it is difficult to see how this would cover the time and effort involved in running a 'normal' diversified portfolio of (say) 20 stocks even if there is no 'cost' involved. This hypothetical investor may decide to invest directly for the educational experience, but it does not make much sense from an economic point of view.

Most unlisted pooled funds have significant initial, sales or up-front charges levied on new investments. To some extent this is offset by the substantially lower acquisition costs paid by investment pools in purchasing listed securities. Up-fronts may seem quite modest, but they are nevertheless a factor. Packaged insurance products often have substantial up-fronts which are not always clearly shown. A fairly simple test of unreasonable up-fronts, which investors can apply for themselves, is to ask any 'adviser' for a written statement of any commissionable interest.

An up-front of (say) 5% is very high for a short-term investment but for a long-term investment which is not expected to be disturbed for 10 years it can be notionally spread over this time and at 0.5% per annum, it does not look unreasonable. Consequently, the reasonableness or otherwise of the up-front will depend to a considerable extent on the nature of the product. One would expect special purpose products such as rollovers, annuities and so on to attract higher up-fronts than their more general counterparts because of the additional work required in meeting the investor's particular needs as far as taxation is concerned.

An ongoing expense of the order of 1.5% per annum is fairly standard. However, the investor should be alert to hidden charges such as a life insurance company investing through in-house unit trusts. In such circumstances it is usual for the ongoing fees to be appropriately adjusted to avoid duplication, but this should be investigated.

The questions of taxation and social security entitlements are both complex and continually changing. These changes and complexities affect the investment environment but they do not alter the fundamental principles.

However, it can be said that generally speaking there are no substantial tax advantages in indirect investment through unit trusts rather than operating directly. Insurance and friendly society bonds need to be assessed for any tax disadvantages. In the case of superannuation, the tax aspects can be important and require specialist advice.

In many cases, taxation issues will dictate to a considerable extent the sort of packaged product which is most appropriate. However, this is only one consideration. The underlying investments, up-fronts and ongoing expenses still require consideration because these matters can negate any tax advantages gained by using a particular class of product.

INVESTMENT POLICY WITH INDIRECT INVESTMENT AND ITS LIMITS

Notwithstanding the convenience (at a price) of indirect investment, it does have its limits. Unless investors are using a packaged product which is specially packaged for taxation purposes, some listed investments may be required to achieve a desired asset allocation.

Some commentators feel that the most important part of investment is asset allocation. An investor who decides that an appropriate long-term policy would be to invest 40% in shares, 30% in listed property trusts and 30% in cash would be able to achieve the desired cash and share component via a number of conventional and conservatively-managed unlisted equity trusts and cash management trusts. However, it may be necessary to venture into the stock market to achieve the desired property component with adequate diversification.

(It is here, incidentally, that there could be a major fallacy in seeking advice from an 'advisory' organisation which is restricted in its scope by regulation or lack of knowledge. For example, a commission-remunerated adviser, who is not employed by a member firm of a stock exchange, risks losing both income and a client in recommending listed securities because the client will need to be referred elsewhere to complete the transaction. One wonders if the practice of issuing restricted dealers' licences was not a significant factor leading to the relative popularity of unlisted property trusts, as distinct from listed ones in the late 1980s — and the subsequent losses.)

Investors who decide to adopt a long-term fixed-asset allocation policy such as that described above would be advised to consider adjustments if there are significant changes in the proportions. Thus, if (as a result of an event such as the speculation prior to the crash of 1987) the equity proportion was to increase considerably, some selling of shares or redemption of equity trust units should be undertaken. However, there are costs involved and this may be unduly expensive for minor changes.

Investors confident of their judgement could adjust their asset allocation according to their analysis of the relative value of the various investment sectors. However there are potential dangers if these adjustments are not made on value but outlook — which is another word for what everyone else thinks. These variations give some scope for producing long-term results which could be better (or worse!) than a 'benchmark' of the results to be obtained by adopting constant proportions in shares, property and cash.

THE SINGLE RESPONSIBLE ENTITY

This discussion of indirect investments would not be complete without discussion of a proposal to eliminate the requirement for independent trustees in some forms of publicly offered collective investment in Australia. This proposal followed from a review conducted by the Australian Law Reform Commission in the early 1990s.[3]

Under this proposal, expected to be implemented in 1998-99, there will no longer be a trustee for unit-holders in various forms of equity trusts, managed funds, etc. Instead, the management company will assume this role as well as its current role of operator and manager of the scheme.

The arguments in favour of this proposal were, broadly:

(a) The current structure is cumbersome and uneconomic

(b) When things go wrong, there are two parties involved which can make it difficult to know who to blame

(c) The existence of the independent trustee did not prevent the disasters of the late 1980s including unlisted property trusts, and Estate Mortgage.

The arguments in favour of retaining an independent trustee are:

(d) The cost is very low compared to management fees

(e) The role of trustees has been misinterpreted; their duty is to ensure that the trust deed is adhered to, not to second-guess the commercial judgement of the management company

(f) While there have been some well publicised failures of trustee companies to discharge their duties, there has been little publicity of the numerous occasions on which trustees have prevented disasters and breaches of trust deeds.

Perhaps it should be noted that government regulation and supervision did not prevent the disasters either. In some cases, official involvement may have had a contrary effect by providing an aura of respectability, such as the 'Trustee Investment' status of Pyramid Building Society.

Villains interested in fleecing the public may find some useful hints in some of the amusing articles which appear in the 'Pierpont' column in the *Australian Financial Review*.[4] It might be worth remembering one of his remarks:

> "... As soon as [the Federal Treasurer] rams through his legislation replacing trustees with a 'single responsible entity', the Pierpont Investment Trust will be poised and waiting like a spider in a web.

> "When it comes to parting investors from their money, it has long been recognised that unit trusts are a far superior mechanism to companies. ..."

In this brave new world of the 'single responsible entity', there may be an argument for investors preferring trusts, funds or schemes which retain long-established and highly-respected managers, an independent trustee or which are subject to the public scrutiny afforded by stock exchange listing.

Chapter 7

Investing in Listed Securities and Unusual Pools

BEFORE WE BEGIN

THERE ARE a number of reasons for operating directly in the stock market rather than indirectly through unlisted and/or packaged products. As we saw in the previous chapter it may be necessary to do so in order to obtain a desired level of property investment with an adequate diversification. Also, there are a number of ways in which an investor may be able to improve upon the purchase of a conservatively-managed conventional equity trust.

Investors who decide that they wish to operate directly should recognise at the outset that, if the object of this choice is to achieve superior results, their task is by no means simple. To quote the former Managing Director of the Save and Prosper Group in the UK:[1]

> "There are extremely astute individuals on both sides of the Atlantic (and on the Continent of Europe) who devote all their time and energy to the investment business with a view to making a profit for themselves or their institutions. The small saver who manages his own investments is competing against these. If he is one of those people whose awareness of what is going on in the market is confined to what he learns by reading the City columns of the daily newspapers coupled with an occasional talk to his stockbroker, he is at a heavy disadvantage when he tries to beat the professionals at their own game."

There are sometimes opportunities which a private investor can exploit with a reasonable expectation of 'beating the professionals'. The first is to purchase shares in listed investment companies which are operated on conventional lines when it is possible to do so at a significant discount on the underlying value of the portfolio. In some cases it may be possible to buy shares in a listed investment company instead of shares in an unlisted trust where there is a common management.

The pursuit of this course of action requires an analysis adequate to ensure that the investment portfolio is run on 'conventional' or 'average' lines by an experienced and conservative team, and this approach is not invalidated by the apparent logic of amateurs foolishly trying to beat professionals at their own game. After all, the managers of one investment company are hardly likely to support the market price of their competitors' companies.

A second approach is to play a different game, recognising that the chief objective of a very significant proportion of the investment community is to be in the top-tier of investment performance surveys which cover relatively short periods. Amateurs (and enlightened superannuation fund trustees whose members permit them to ignore investment performance surveys) do not suffer from this disadvantage and can devote their efforts to producing good long-term results.

It will quickly become apparent that the further investors venture along the road of direct investment the more attention they will need to devote to annual reports and financial statements.

The reader will recall from Chapter 1 the extensive investigations by John Train which suggested three methods of producing superior results. Briefly they were:

(a) Value-oriented investing

(b) Long-term holding of outstanding growth stocks

(c) Finding a new investment area.

DEFENSIVE AND ENTERPRISING INVESTORS

In *The Intelligent Investor*, Graham described two types of 'value-investors'. The first type, defensive investors, are the genuinely amateur investors who understand security values but are unable or unwilling to devote substantial time and effort to their investments. For these people Graham suggested a diet of large conservatively-operated companies purchased at reasonable prices. These investors should be happy with reasonable results, not expect the impossible and should probably restrict their activities to the 100 largest companies in Australia and avoid mining stocks.

For enterprising investors — those who are willing and able to devote substantial amounts of time, study and effort into analysing securities with the intention of exploiting differences between price and value — the diet can be widened. However, there are problems in departing from the defensive investor's diet. Apart from anything else investors will need to do their own research, and will not usually be able to rely on the work of brokers' analysts. The fact that smaller companies are less actively followed by broking houses means that this class of company is more likely to offer a big differential between price and value. This makes the field more fertile for those with the ability and inclination to do the research — but it also makes it more dangerous for those who are unable or lack the time to conduct a thorough analysis.

According to Graham's definition of the difference between investment and speculation, it could therefore be argued that investors who operate in the domain of the enterprising investor when they lack the time, knowledge, interest, inclination or experience are *ipso facto* speculating.

Selecting 'growth' opportunities before such companies' outstanding prospects are reflected in the share price and finding a whole new investment area are two activities which are very definitely in the realm of the enterprising investor. Would-be enterprising investors will wish to make an extensive study of this subject and in consequence their educational and experience requirements are considerable. Those who wish to discover a whole new investment area should not expect to find any clues here, although their search will be shortened by knowing methods and approaches which are unlikely to work.

Value-oriented investing is itself becoming harder as the ideas become better known — a point noted by Train in *The New Money Masters* (his second edition). Despite these difficulties, this chapter attempts to present some investment options for those who wish to attempt direct investment in listed securities. However, it should be recognised that the suggestions are made with the requirements of the genuinely amateur defensive investor in mind.

Most people who invest directly in the stock market have usually achieved that status in a haphazard way. For example, they may have started buying on a 'tip' from a friend, they may have bought shares in the company they work for, they may have inherited some shares from a relative, subscribed to a 'privatisation' issue or they may have read a book about investment and decided to try it out.

Unfortunately, the selection of individual securities can never be taught entirely from a book. It has to be learned by actual practice, with the investor's hard-earned savings at risk. Only then will the investor experience the psychological factors of disappointment, success and crowd behaviour which are so important. Consequently, these direct investment options are presented in an order that most people will find easiest to put into practice.

LISTED PROPERTY TRUSTS

For the novice investor, property trusts are probably the easiest listed security to start with for a number of reasons:

(a) There are only a handful to consider — most sharebrokers should be able to supply a complete list without too much trouble. Alternatively, complete lists are published regularly in the financial press.

(b) The accounts are far easier to understand than company reports. Also most annual reports contain a complete list of the properties owned by the trust which enables investors to form their own opinion on the quality of the properties — by inspection if necessary.

(c) Finally, investors can usually satisfy their needs for cash investments and ordinary shares using cash management production and listed investment companies or unlisted equity trusts, but investment in individual listed property trusts will often be required to complete a balanced portfolio.

As with most forms of listed investment the number of securities on offer usually exceeds the investor's needs or research capacity. It is not possible to read every report and study every balance sheet in detail. Consequently, there is a need to whittle the complete list down to a manageable short-list for detailed investigation.

There is no ideal way of establishing a short-list and there is always the risk that any hard and fast rule will eliminate some potentially excellent investments. However, investors who are new to the business should probably start by investigating the largest half dozen (or so) trusts by market capitalisation.

The investor should be seeking to obtain, at reasonable prices, a beneficial interest in investment property, spread both geographically and by type of property. The principal types of property are offices and retail complexes, although some trusts may also contain business 'parks', car parks, factories and warehouses.

To a very large extent assessing the property portfolios of these trusts requires careful reading of the annual reports and a good dose of common sense. Investors who wish to opt for a minimum of fuss could perhaps concentrate their investment in a few diversified trusts. There may be some advantages in holding smaller investments in trusts which are dominated by properties of a particular type or in a particular geographical location, but the 1990s vacancy problems in office buildings (particularly in Melbourne, Adelaide and Perth) demonstrate the dangers of holding a portfolio which, in aggregate, is not properly diversified.

Diversification is an aggregate requirement, achieved by holding a number of investments. For example, an investment portfolio which holds similar amounts in one trust which owns a geographically-spread list of shopping complexes and in a second trust containing a geographical spread of office buildings would be reasonably diversified even though each of the individual trusts, by themselves, was not diversified by type of property.

Listed property trusts are not companies. Investors rights and entitlements are defined in a trust deed to which there will normally be two other parties. The trustee is usually responsible for ensuring that all the legal requirements of the trust deed are complied with and holds title to the assets of the trust. The manager of the trust is usually responsible for managing the assets of the trust and initiating investment decisions. There is also the question of unit-holder liability, which, although most trusts have taken great pains to avoid, should be noted. Most prospectuses usually say something like:[2]

> "*Although the legal position is somewhat uncertain, the Trust Deed contains provisions which the Manager believes are adequate, based on the present case law in Australia, to limit the liability of unitholders against claims by either the Trustee or third parties...*"

The debacle in the unlisted property trust market in the early 1990s led to a great deal of criticism of trustee companies who, with the benefit of hindsight, had not done enough to protect investors from poor decisions made by managers. It is important to note therefore that, in general, trustees have tended to go along with the commercial decisions of trust managers — and would need a fairly good reason, beyond a difference of commercial judgement, to knock back a manager's proposal which complied with the trust deed and any other legal requirements.

In consequence, the quality and integrity of the manager of any listed trust is of vital importance to any potential investor. In so far as integrity is concerned, there is always the problem identified in Chapter 5 of the manager having an interest in increasing the number of units on issue while this may not be in the interest of investors — particularly if the issue dilutes their investment. Suspension of distribution reinvestment plans during depressed periods is a very definite plus-factor in assessing the priority with which the manager acts in the interests of unit-holders.

In the past, a couple of managers of small trusts built up significant stakes of their own in the trust they managed (either directly or in the name of an associate) and then sold this stake to a new organisation which was subsequently appointed manager of the trust. Investors should be wary of organisations which have in the past been party to such transactions and where the outgoing manager/unit-holder has not insisted on fellow unit-holders receiving a comparable offer.

Professional fund management organisations rely a great deal on establishing a history of fair dealing with their clients. An organisation which conducts any transactions which benefits itself at the expense of its clients will probably be suffered in silence at the time but may find it impossible to regain the trust which is so essential to progress. Investors should therefore pay close attention to the history of the management of the trust and the directors of the management company. This will be more important in the future than it has been in the past with the move towards a *single responsible entity*.

Before leaving the question of manager, there is also the question of whether the manager's fees are reasonable or otherwise. This is not always straightforward as some managers absorb expenses which in other cases are paid by the trust. Total fees and expenses under 1% per annum of the value of the trust are reasonable. Fees and expenses in excess of 1.5% per annum would require further thought.

Finally, there is the question of price. Generally, the properties of listed trusts are revalued regularly. In this respect investors need to recognise that essentially these valuations are *estimates* of market values. This does not necessarily coincide with an investor's time frame. While properties are usually valued on the basis of sale within a reasonable time the investor should be purchasing units in listed trusts with a view to long-term holding — 10 years or more.

In depressed times, the prices of listed trust units will often trade at significant discounts on the net asset value per unit. In buoyant times, the price may exceed net asset value by a considerable margin. This would suggest that such units should not be bought at more than a modest premium above net asset value per unit (say 1.1 times) unless there is good reason to believe that the net asset value is grossly understated. Similarly, property investors should expect a reasonable income return on their investment — perhaps a minimum of 7% per annum on the purchase price after adjusting for anticipated vacancies in the following two years. These are minimum criteria and investors should normally expect to do somewhat better.

Let us now suppose that an investor has selected six listed trusts which seem to contain reasonably-located property, are well-managed, meet the other criteria discussed above and are available at reasonable prices. The next step is to check the investor's diversification — by calculating on paper the overall spread by type of property and geographical location and the amount of a portfolio exposed to any one property.

Finally, the investor should consider the legislative risk. From time to time politicians and civil servants see trusts as mechanisms for avoiding tax. The trusts to which they refer are principally family discretionary trusts rather than public unit trusts such as cash management trusts, equity trusts, managed funds and listed property trusts. However, there is always some risk that unit-holders of the latter, who are generally people of modest means, will be unintentionally caught up in some future attack on trusts directed at tax avoidance.

'CONVENTIONAL' INVESTMENT COMPANIES

A conventional investment company is an organisation, the principal activity of which is the purchase and indefinite retention of a portfolio of shares which roughly matches market indices as far as individual securities are concerned.

It is sometimes possible to purchase securities in such companies at substantial discounts on the value of the underlying investments. The principal objection to this course is the unknown discount on underlying asset value at the time of eventual sale, and in consequence many investors prefer equity trusts which can always be redeemed at net asset value.

Until quite recently, most investment companies only had to meet the expenses of its directors and staff and as a result the expenses were often considerably less than the corresponding costs associated with the operation of a trust. In the last 10 years, there has been a tendency for investment companies to be promoted by fund managers who receive a fee of the order of 1% per annum for managing the investments of the listed company.

The combination of lower annual expenses, where this is the case, and purchase at a discount will often make the purchase of 'conventional' listed investment companies more attractive that unlisted equity trusts. It is perhaps unfortunate that such a 'recommendation' may be outside the permitted scope of some advisers' licences.

However, this is a field which is always worth investigation because, depending on the discount, it may be possible to 'beat the professionals at their own game' with very little effort by purchasing the professionals' own $1 chips for only 80 cents.

If this course is chosen, investors should obtain and study the latest annual report. The board must be conservative and err on the dull side. Ideally, the senior executive team should all have established records in the industry of at least 10 years (and preferably 20 years) in conservative institutions. Changes in management, the appointment of 'whiz-kids' to the board, or the sudden appearance of sporting heroes with no investment expertise in senior management positions should be viewed with suspicion.

The purpose of this exercise is to acquire at a significant discount shares in a company whose underlying assets will produce roughly average results. If these shares are not purchased at a discount in the first place, there is always the risk of loss — in addition to adverse stock market movements — if it becomes necessary to make a subsequent sale at a discount.

One other aspect of the discount is the provision which an investment company makes for tax on realised capital gains. Practice varies from one company to another. If it is possible to buy shares in listed companies at a price that is less than net asset value (after allowing for tax on unrealised capital gains) and the company is a very passive investor, investors in the company will gain the benefit of any earnings on this provision until such time as the need for it materialises.

While investment via listed investment companies will achieve diversification in terms of the underlying securities, overall control is still vested in one management team. Diversification for the investor therefore remains an issue despite the diversified nature of the underlying investments. Perhaps the amount invested in any one investment company could be larger than the amount which investors would contemplate investing in any individual trading company but the old rule about not placing too many eggs in one basket still applies.

UNFASHIONABLE LARGE COMPANIES

Investors who wish to venture beyond the realm of conventional investment companies could consider, as their next option, investment in unfashionable large companies. In the first two chapters, the dangers of following investment fashions were emphasised. This then leads to the question as to whether it is possible to achieve above average investment results by deliberately purchasing shares in large companies which are unpopular among professional investors and the sharebroking fraternity. At a later stage the question of secondary companies will be considered.

What then is the definition of large as distinct from small or secondary? It is easy to fix an arbitrary figure such as shareholders' funds in excess of $200 million — but one purpose of this distinction between secondary and large is to differentiate between companies which are sufficiently large and widely held to be regularly researched by sharebrokers' analysts. Secondary companies are those which require detailed research by the investor.

Generally speaking the largest 100 companies are regularly analysed. Some companies outside this definition are also widely followed and researched which makes it difficult to draw a line with any accuracy.

For the purposes of this discussion, it might be reasonable to say that stocks outside the top 200 companies are secondary and those in the range 100 to 200 could be classified either way depending on the investor's access to research material.

An important aspect of this restriction is that the investor should be able to obtain quality research reports on large companies from most of the medium to large broking firms. For reasons already discussed, the usual buy-hold-sell recommendations on these reports should be treated with caution. (Apart from anything else some firms define a 'buy' as a security whose price is expected to produce above average performance in the next 12 months. This is hardly the time frame for a genuine long-term investor.)

The market thrives on prospective price/earnings ratios and the 'outlook for growth'. A great deal of research is devoted to estimating company profits one or two years hence. Relatively less importance is paid to dividend yields. Net asset values per share are often not mentioned.

These value indicators are all linked by profitability (the rate of after-tax return on shareholders' funds) and payout ratios (the proportion of profits distributed as dividends). For example, a company with a net asset value of $2 per share may make a profit of 10% on shareholders' funds or 20 cents per share. Typically such a company would pay out approximately 60% of this profit by way of dividends or 12 cents per share. If the share price is $3 then:

(a) The dividend yield is 4%

(b) The price/earnings ratio is 15

(c) The ratio of market price/net-assets value is 1.5.

Unfortunately, such perfect examples rarely occur in practice. If the company is doing well its profitability may be (say) 20% in which case it would be earning 40 cents per share and at $3 the price/earnings ratio would be 7.5. It is here that one of the great dangers of the price/earnings ratio is obvious. Continuing profitability of 20% on shareholders' funds is probably an unreasonable expectation and consequently there should be some doubt as to whether a valuation based on this level of earnings would be sound. In such circumstances a company board who understood their business would probably only increase the dividend slightly to (say) 14 cents per share.

Conversely, let us assume that the company is having a difficult time and earning only 5% on shareholders' funds or 10 cents per share. In such circumstances the directors may decide to maintain the 12 cents dividend (using accumulated reserves) in the expectation of a recovery. It is most likely that the share price will also be depressed in these circumstances. Provided the share price is depressed and the company's difficulties are temporary, investors will do well from purchasing the shares at these depressed levels.

This is the essential principle on which the success of value-oriented investing depends. It is not extremely difficult but it does require a little research. The first requirement is a simple formula which quickly identifies potential candidates for further analysis. Many people rely on price/earnings ratios, but this often eliminates good companies in temporary difficulties. Bearing in mind the tendency of company boards to maintain dividends in temporarily difficult times, using dividend yield would be better. A screen based on both dividend yield and the ratio of market price to net assets is probably the most effective.

Investors who wish to try this method could start by listing all the top 100 companies (excluding property trusts) with dividend yields of 6% or more whose share price is not more than 1.1 times asset backing. At the present time — November 1997 — the likely result is a blank sheet of paper! This will not always be the case.

Inclusion on such a list does not automatically mean that a company's shares are worth buying; neither does exclusion mean that a company's shares are not worth buying. This is merely a procedure for identifying potential candidates for further analysis.

The second requirement is to ensure that the company's difficulties are only temporary. Sometimes this may be obvious and sometimes not. Here it is important to look at the company's trading record over an extended period of years paying particular attention to operating profit in relation to turnover and shareholders' funds.

The third requirement is to ensure that the company is soundly financed and competently managed. This involves, *inter alia*, investigation of the relationship between current assets and liabilities, and total assets to shareholders' funds.

An investor relying on someone else's analysis should be satisfied that these issues are addressed.

Finally, investors operating in this way must accept the possibility of mistakes — by the company's directors in preparing its financial statements, by the analyst conducting the research, by themselves in misjudging the company's prospects or difficulties. (The possibility of deliberate accounting errors or 'creative' accounting should also be borne in mind.) Diversification is vital and if the construction of such a list only produces one or two companies, investors should think twice about proceeding because it is possible that the market as a whole is grossly overpriced and the good may well 'die with the bad'. For this reason some assessment of the overall market should be used in conjunction with these methods.

SECONDARY COMPANIES

As already noted, the essential difference between primary and secondary stocks, from the point of view of amateur investors, is that they will have to conduct their own research. Reliable analyses from other sources will not always be available.

One of the benefits of finding undervalued primary companies in temporary difficulties is that, once the problems have been overcome, the greater market-following will make it more likely for the improvement to be reflected in the share price. On the other hand, undervaluation in secondary companies may go unnoticed for long periods and a great deal of patience may be required.

Nevertheless, secondary securities should be a happy hunting ground for those with the necessary time and skills for a number of reasons:

(a) Such companies are not actively traded, consequently they are less actively followed by brokers' analysts which increases the possibility of large discrepancies between price and value.

(b) Smaller companies are more likely to be taken over than large companies. In such circumstances the bidding company usually offers a price which is very satisfactory to the shareholders of the company being acquired.

(c) The vulnerability to takeover helps concentrate the minds of directors and management on the priority which they allocate to the interests of shareholders in their deliberations.

UNUSUAL POOLS

Investors who wish to benefit from exposure to secondary companies, but who lack the time or interest in detailed analysis, could consider purchasing shares in specialist investment companies or some other indirect investment medium.

This does require close attention to the investment policy of the organisation and the competence of those involved in its implementation. The findings of John Train suggest those policies which are likely to be successful in the long run and those which are not.

The next step is to examine the activities of the portfolio to be satisfied that the stated policy is in fact being carried out. For example, a value-oriented investment company should be able to demonstrate that its investments represent good value. The portfolio may contain a few mistakes but commitment to the stated policy must be established.

Competence of the management of an unusual pool also needs to be assessed. This assessment needs to be conducted in relation to the proposed investment policy. For example, selection of 'cheap' secondary companies requires quite different skills to the selection of 'growth opportunities'. Successful investors come from a variety of backgrounds, nevertheless common sense would suggest that extensive and relevant experience is essential.

The research effort and expertise involved in operating a specialised and/or unusual investment pool may justify higher operating expenses than normal. However, there is no point in investing in such a pool if the extra expenses are so high as to offset any benefit to be derived from the investment policy.

Finally, there is the influence of investment performance on the perceptions of potential investors to consider. The combination of an unusual investment policy and 'performance'-based promotion has often brought disappointment to many investors.

EVERY INVESTOR HAS A SPEED LIMIT

No matter how much we tried, very few of us could ever run a mile in four minutes. We are not built for it. However, with instruction and practice most of us are capable of handling a car (on a suitable track) at speeds of 130 kilometres per hour.

Running a marathon will not have universal appeal even though most people could get there in the end given enough time and encouragement. But most people would have neither the interest or time for such an event. Similarly, investors who dislike figures or reading financial statements may need to admit that detailed analysis is not their cup of tea, even if they could expect to get there in the end.

Those with the necessary ability and not the interest are in the same boat as those without the necessary knowledge. Such investors may expose themselves to less risk if they are frank with themselves about the limitations imposed by their lack of time and/or interest and pursue investment methods with which they are comfortable.

There are a number of good books available for those wishing to learn how to conduct their own research. One specifically written with Australian investors in mind is Martin Roth's *Analysing Company Accounts*[3]. However, there is a limit to how much can be learned from books. Investing on the stock market is a practical skill.

In many ways learning to invest is like learning to fly a small aeroplane — it appears daunting and requires a combination of theoretical learning and recent practice to remain proficient. But given the necessary time and effort (and money), this is a skill most people could acquire.

However, the analogy with flying goes further. Different levels of skill and experience are required for handling more difficult tasks. The same applies in the investment world, accepting one's limitations may place limits on the results which can be achieved, but it also helps restrict the disappointments.

Chapter 8

Theoretical Principles and Considerations

THE NEED FOR A 'NEW' INVESTMENT THEORY?

THIS CHAPTER is principally written for professional investors and others who are interested in the scientific development of a theoretical framework or model which describes the behaviour of capital markets and their participants.

While describing short-term market behaviour in terms of volatility may be helpful for professional option traders and short-term speculators, long-term behaviour would be better described relative to traditional accounting data which itself needs to be modelled over time. By dissecting asset performance in this way, the results are more reliable and the relationships between cause and effect correspond more closely with the 'real' world. This is the essence of the argument which follows.

Although individual investors may profit from grossly inefficient markets, inefficiencies distort the allocation of resources within a community and, in extreme cases such as 1929 (and 1997?) in the USA, can cause widespread misery for many years to come. Consequently, there is a need for greater efficiency and more rational capital markets, for the benefit of the community as a whole as well as the investing public.

The advantage of a valid theoretical framework or model is its invocation of scientific method. In his book on this subject,[1] Patrick

Rivett, Professor of Operational Research at the University of Sussex wrote in 1971:

"All scientists are aware that the central act of the scientific method is the creation of a model."

It may well be that scientific method has no place in investment markets. But that should not prevent an attempt. As testament to the interest in this development are the numerous articles on theoretical aspects of portfolio management which appear in JASSA, the Journal of the Securities Institute of Australia, and in corresponding investment professionals' publications throughout the world as well as academic periodicals such as *Journal of Finance*.

It is now becoming apparent that a great deal of this work in the past has been wasted on a theory which was built on assumptions which have turned out to be quicksand. To avoid a repetition, it might be worthwhile reflecting on the saga of what became known as 'Modern Portfolio Theory' before continuing.

In 1995, Robert Haugen, Professor of Finance at the University of California, Irvine, published a book which 'makes the case for the inefficient market.'[2] He begins his concluding remarks by pointing out that the idea of efficient markets originated with an observation that percentage changes in large stocks appeared to be uncorrelated.

The lack of correlation suggested that price movements in one period were independent of what had happened in the past. While independent variables are uncorrelated, it is a huge jump in logic to infer independence from lack of significant correlation.

To begin with, being unable to establish non-zero correlation does not prove that the correlation is zero. Secondly, zero correlation is not **sufficient** to establish independence. Nevertheless, independence of price movements was tentatively assumed and most of the model development was dictated by theoretical arguments and 'logical' assumptions, as a result of which academics:[3]

".... spent 30 years bending and twisting the data and then the theories, trying to make them sing in harmony.

... But most of the major advances in human knowledge did not follow an arrow running through the theories into the empirical tests. Rather **most of our greatest triumphs proceeded in the opposite direction from data to theory.** *.... "*

The history of science is full of discredited theories which were based on argument rather than observation such as the idea that the speed at which objects fell would depend on their weight. This theory was debated at length by philosophers until Galileo dropped two different weights from the Tower of Pisa and discredited the theory.

Much the same can be said of efficient market theory. It was partly developed from plausible, but invalid, assumptions such as rational investor behaviour. Haugen summarises the problem succinctly:[4]

*"We have now seen the results of many straightforward attempts to document the behaviour of stock prices. These results do not conform to the predictions of the theories. **They don't even come close.**"*

How then did these theories become so entrenched? To quote Haugen again:

"We in finance – did we not embrace our theories too quickly? Before learning how financial markets behave? Do we not embrace them now too tenaciously in the face of growing criticism that our fidelity is unfounded?"

Haugen identifies one cause of the problem — that academia, on the whole, did not bother to check all of the underlying facts and assumptions on which its theories were based. This points to a breakdown in communication between 'town' and 'gown' on this matter.

Few practitioners of 20 years ago had the necessary academic training to challenge the arguments in a language which academia understood. This made it easy for academics to dismiss criticism by saying 'your grasp of this concept is inadequate to justify further discussion'. Academia assumed a position of superiority in its own eyes and, in the process, displayed an element of arrogance. Practitioners with decades of experience had learnt to treat investment theories with a grain of salt. The confident attitude with which academic circles proclaimed their new theories did not help communication either. Alan Geddes recalls:[5]

"The two sides met at a seminar run by the Australian Society of Security Analysts at Macquarie University in February 1973, and

*although at the time they annoyed each other intensely, they are still
talking about the encounter and looking forward to the next
confrontation."*

The undergraduate courses on offer, the development of trading in
financial derivatives, the competition amongst professional investors
looking for ideas which give them an advantage and the ready
availability of powerful desktop computers brought new types of
professional people into the market who wanted to use their
knowledge. Included in this crop of graduate recruits were a number of
people with highly developed and advanced mathematical skills
respectfully known as 'rocket scientists'.

With time these former students acquired some practical experience.
The net result was a significant increase in the number of people with
both practical experience and academic training. These people could
understand — and challenge — academically fashionable capital market
theories. 'Anomalies' began to be documented in the peculiar language
of these theories and, in some quarters, 'anomaly' documentation has
turned to outright criticism of the whole package. 'Paper' bricks have
begun to fly in both directions!

For example in 1996, the Faculty of Actuaries in Scotland held a
meeting to discuss a paper from a practitioner which was highly critical
of modern portfolio theory or 'financial economics' as he called it.[6] The
meeting was addressed by a number of practitioners and academics.
Judging from the edited transcript of the discussion, the meeting was
extremely lively.

Haugen is not the only university professor to suggest that the root
cause of the problem has been an unwillingness within the academic
world to listen to practitioners and other critics. Gordon Pepper, well
known in the United Kingdom as both an academic and investment
practitioner in the government securities market, listened to the
discussion at the Faculty of Actuaries meeting and subsequently wrote
as follows:[7]

*"In many disciplines there is a general tendency for academics to
specialise; but to be a 'good specialist' you need to be a 'good generalist',
in order to keep the specialisation in perspective. As the depth of
knowledge becomes greater, people may be forced to specialise in
progressively narrower fields. The result can be that they become very*

narrow minded and lose their perspective. Further, there is a tendency to build layer upon layer of complication on top of basic assumptions that are approximations. The result is an inverted pyramid on top of dubious foundations. As an intellectual exercise it may be very clever, but it has lost touch with reality. The academics would do much better to re-examine the foundations, secure them and rebuild the pyramid. The difficulty is that they may have become so blinkered that they are incapable of doing so. Anyone querying the foundations is attacking their field of specialisation, which will become obsolete if the attack is successful. If this happens, the academics will become redundant if they are incapable of changing fields. Not surprisingly, they try to defend themselves."

In so far as the current debate over Modern Portfolio Theory is concerned, it seems that Rivett, writing in 1971,[8] was almost clairvoyant:

"*Model construction is an amalgam of theory and practice in which, unfortunately, either theory or practice appears from time to time as the dominant constituent. When theory is dominant, elegance of mathematical exposition may lead to consequences which are incapable of implementation. On the other hand hurried problem solving which conceals within it a technical ineptitude may mean that insight into the structure is lost. Between these two extremes there lies a depopulated no man's land. A false distinction and a sham battle between the 'pure' and 'applied' has meant that the pure have applied their theories and the applied their practice, in two different incommunicating languages.*"

From the point of view of academia, the answer as to whether a new investment theory is required is clearly 'yes', for the very practical and self-interested reason that the existing theory is headed for the scrap heap and without something to replace it large numbers of finance academics may need to find another occupation.

The principal practical advantage of a valid investment model would be to place the investment process on a scientific footing within the design limits and validity of the model. Practitioners would also benefit from this because the 'structure' would give them greater confidence in predicting the consequences of numerous everyday decisions.

One example is the relative performance of Australian industrial stocks compared to resources stocks over the period 1980 to 1996 discussed earlier. If a general scientific model explained this phenomenon, then a case could be made for avoiding resources stocks as a group — unless there is a substantial change to the basis on which their shares are priced.

Similar comments apply to the correlation between investment return and the price-to-book ratio or the price/net-assets ratio as it is more commonly known in Australia. If a rational explanation for this phenomenon follows from a valid model, then there may be a scientific basis for subsequent action. Consider, for example, security analysts' reports. Few of these mention, yet alone feature, the price/net-assets ratio — now believed to be the single most important fundamental factor in assessing future relative market performance.[9]

It is also possible that a valid model would provide central bankers with sound evidence when capital markets indicate that there is something seriously wrong with the economy, of which US market valuations of 1997 are a clear symptom. The history of this particular bubble and its aftermath should make fascinating reading when the dust has settled!

MEASURING PRICE FLUCTUATIONS RELATIVE TO ACCOUNTING DATA

Although a great deal is unknown about the statistical form of short-term movements, the central assumption of independence seems to be sufficiently accurate for option pricing models based on 'efficient market' theory to have worn the test of time.

However, the extrapolation of this 'efficient market' approach into longer term problems has not worked. As the time period increases the number of approximately independent variables which constitute the whole price movement increases and the underlying assumption of independence breaks down.

In *Chaos and Order in the Capital Markets*, Edgar Peters[10] uses a statistic known as the 'Hurst coefficient' to demonstrate that stock price trends tend to persist much more than would be the case if price movements in successive time periods were unrelated. It also appears that the variance of stock index movements in Australia, the USA and the United Kingdom over intervals of 10 years or more is less than half of what would be expected if this assumption of independence were valid.[11]

Skilled mathematicians have focused considerable intellectual firepower on this problem and have proposed numerous explanations involving highly sophisticated ideas such as fluctuating variance (auto-regressive conditional heteroscedasticity) and complex (fractal) probability distributions. This 'rocket science' may improve the formulae used by short-term speculators, arbitragers and option traders but investors should have longer horizons. Sooner or later they need to consider market prices in relation to balance sheets and other fundamentals such as profits and dividends.

It is perhaps unfortunate that so much investment theory has been based on the statistical properties of market price movements in isolation from company financial statements. An alternative approach is to reconsider market prices relative to traditional measures of corporate value and, instead of investigating price movements, to investigate fluctuations in (say) price/earnings ratios.

For example, we can think of the relationship between a company's share price n years hence, P_n, in terms of earnings per share n years hence, E_n, and the corresponding values today as follows:

$$\frac{P_n}{P_o} = \frac{P_n}{E_n} \times \frac{E_n}{E_o} \times \frac{E_o}{P_o}$$

If this expression is reorganised by reversing the order of the last two terms, inverting the second term and dividing instead of multiplying, we arrive at the following:

$$\frac{P_n}{P_o} = \left\{ \frac{P_n}{E_n} \div \frac{P_o}{E_o} \right\} \times \frac{E_n}{E_o}$$

In words, the price n years' hence in relation to the price today is equal to the price/earnings ratio n years' hence divided by the price/earnings ratio today multiplied by the earnings per share n years' hence divided by the earnings per share today.

Now the price/earnings ratio today and the earnings per share are known. The unknown elements are the price/earnings ratio n years' hence and the growth in earnings per share in the interim. This may sound like substituting two unknown variables for one, but past fluctuations in price/earnings ratios and growth in earnings per share have been much less variable than prices in isolation.

There is a widely held belief that it is impossible to forecast future price/earnings ratios and growth in earnings per share[12] with any accuracy. We could therefore assume that these figures tend to converge to a market mean. Although this is not a particularly reliable estimate, it may be the best estimate available. If this view is valid, even approximately, then future price performance would depend inversely on the price/earnings ratio today.

Although the earnings per share measure has been used to demonstrate what is meant by measuring price fluctuations relative to balance sheet fundamentals, other per share measures such as dividends, book value, cash flow or sales could be used. In the United Kingdom, a working party of The Institute of Actuaries concerned with the adequacy of reserves for maturity guarantees on endowment policies used a dividend transformation as the basis of their recommendations.[13]

Alternatively, we can use a book (or net assets) value transformation as the basis of analysis of price changes. If B_t is the book value per share at time t we arrive at the following:

$$\frac{P_n}{P_o} = \left\{ \frac{P_n}{B_n} \div \frac{P_o}{B_o} \right\} \times \frac{B_n}{B_o}$$

There have been numerous studies covering the relationship between price/earnings ratios[14], dividend yields[15] and price-to-book ratios with subsequent relative performance.[16] Does not this simple transformation of measuring price relative to one of the traditional value indicators, coupled with an assumption that growth and the future value indicators are unpredictable, explain the results of these studies, at least partially?

PROFITABILITY IS THE KEY

In the long run, it is balance sheets and profit and loss accounts that provide the foundations which investors and analysts interpret to drive markets. To this rational behaviour, we must then add the ingredients of fads and fashions and the periodic bouts of insanity identified in

Chapter 2. If we wish to understand how markets behave, we first need to understand how corporations and balance sheets behave.

Generally speaking, companies which are growing faster than the market as a whole tend to command above average price/earnings ratios and growth goes hand in hand with profitability. These relationships may not be justified, but influential practitioners use them. To understand how markets behave, we therefore need to understand the fundamental importance of return on capital or profitability.

Profitability is important for three main reasons:

(a) It is the relative profitability of individual firms, industries and economies which enables firms, industries and economies to service debt and attract equity capital. Also within an economy, it is the profitability of the corporate sector which enables it to attract new equity capital from investors who have other options available such as fixed-interest securities and property.

(b) Although this is not well documented, there tends to be a positive relationship between profitability and the price at which a company's shares trade, as measured by dividend yield, price/earnings ratio[17] or the ratio of price to net assets per share.

(c) Ignoring stock market fluctuations for the moment, the underlying source of investor returns is profits, whether distributed as dividends, retained to finance growth or used for stock buy-backs. And profits depend directly on profitability and capital employed.

To determine the relationship between profitability and return to investors, let us start with a common situation in unlisted companies. Small business proprietors sometimes seek 'silent' partners to subscribe equity capital when establishing a company to run the business. This company is then liquidated on termination of the business.

Some of the profits would be distributed by way of dividends, and some would be retained to finance the growth of the business. Alternatively, at one extreme all of the profits could be distributed by way of dividends; at the other extreme all of the profits could be left within the company to be distributed on liquidation.

Irrespective of the dividend policy of this small company, the average rate of compound return achieved on capital subscribed by silent partners over the life of the business will be equal to the average compound rate of return on shareholders' funds. That is to say, the rate of return achieved by investors is equal to the profitability of the business.

Complications in the application of this simple formula arise when the price at which shares are acquired (and sold) is not equal to the book or net asset value of the shares. In the case of small businesses this would be the subject of negotiation; in the case of listed companies prices at or close to net asset value are unusual.

Listed companies often have a dividend policy which may be explicitly stated or inferred from historical patterns with the remainder of profits retained to finance growth. It is relatively easy to demonstrate[18] that, given a constant level of return on shareholders' funds or profitability *pr* and a constant proportion of profits paid in dividends *pd* then shareholders' funds, earnings and dividends will grow at *pr* x *(1 – pd)* compound.

THE INVERTED DIVIDEND DISCOUNT MODEL

One approach to the valuation of ordinary shares is to observe that if the current dividend is **dps** per share, dividends grow at **dg** per annum and **vr** is the valuation discount rate, then the present value of the dividend stream for every share is:

$$\frac{dps}{\{vr - dg\}}$$

This formula is a simplified version of what is commonly known as the dividend discount model.

Unfortunately, the application of this formula is fraught with danger because, when the valuation discount rate **vr** and the assumed dividend growth rate **dg** are close, the result is highly sensitive to minor changes in these assumptions. Also, when they are equal, the valuation is infinite.

However, the model can be inverted and used to answer a different question — what is the return that investors will achieve by buying shares at the present price **Px** and holding them indefinitely. By equating the value of the dividend stream with the price and solving for the valuation discount rate we obtain:

$$vr = \frac{dps}{Px} + dg$$

Now ***dps / Px*** is the dividend yield and, on the assumptions set out in the previous section (i.e. constant profitability and payout ratio), we can derive the simple formula that, as a first approximation, the return which investors can expect from a share they buy and hold indefinitely is equal to:

➤ the *dividend yield* at the time of purchase, *plus*

➤ the *profitability* of the company *multiplied* by the *proportion of profits retained.*

To estimate the long-term return from buy and hold strategies, theorists have traditionally used historical price and dividend data. However, stock price history is very volatile. Profitability is also volatile, but a great deal less volatile than percentage stock price movements. Consequently, an estimate based on profitability will be more reliable than one based on stock price history.

The use of profitability and payout ratios, while perfect in theory, presents problems in practice for a number of reasons. Companies normally report profitability in two ways. In the first instance abnormal and extraordinary items are excluded. Abnormal and extraordinary items, while irregular, are sometimes very large and often negative and, to complicate matters further, the definition of abnormal and extraordinary changes from time to time with accounting protocols. The figure for 'return of equity' quoted by companies normally excludes abnormal extraordinary items. In the case of banks, bad debts are considered part of normal business even though a layman might regard the problems of the late 1980s as 'abnormal'.

PRACTICAL ESTIMATION OF PROFITABILITY AND PAYOUT RATIOS

Here is the reported profitability of seven prominent Australian companies for their last six financial years as set out in their annual reports. The figures for ANZ Bank are only shown on an 'after abnormals' basis in the table overleaf:

Profitability Excluding Abnormal Items (% per annum)

	1991	1992	1993	1994	1995	1996	Av
Amcor	9.6	11.2	11.7	12.2	13.8	11.0	11.6
BHP	15.7	11.0	11.2	12.6	13.6	10.7	12.4
Boral	9.8	6.7	9.6	8.9	10.4	7.2	8.6
CSR	11.6	6.7	7.4	9.6	11.8	9.4	9.4
Pac. Dunlop	17.6	10.6	12.1	13.1	11.4	9.2	12.3
Santos	9.7	13.2	13.4	8.8	9.9	12.3	11.2
Average							**10.9**

Profitability After Abnormal and Extraordinary Items (% per annum)

	1991	1992	1993	1994	1995	1996	Av
Amcor	12.8	13.4	13.8	9.3	12.3	10.4	12.4
ANZ Bank	5.8	-11.4	5.0	15.6	17.9	18.3	8.5
BHP	19.1	6.8	13.5	12.6	10.2	8.6	11.8
Boral	9.8	6.7	9.6	4.4	10.4	7.2	8.0
CSR	11.5	-14.7	8.1	9.6	11.9	9.7	6.0
Pac. Dunlop	17.6	8.8	11.5	12.3	3.9	-6.1	8.0
Santos	-9.4	9.1	15.9	12.4	7.3	12.3	7.6
Average							**8.9**

The fluctuation in profitability is an important question. Average profitability before abnormals is typically around 10% per annum and CSR and Boral would be disappointed with their profitability over this period. It also appears that a company should be expected to have a big loss once in every ten years or so. This suggests that investors should assume 'normal' profitability of around 11% per annum and deduct 1% per annum for unexpected losses to arrive at 10% per annum as a long-term estimate.

A related issue is the fluctuation in payout ratio. Company boards do not determine their dividends by applying a standard payout ratio to their profits every year. If a company has had a significant profit increase the dividend is often increased a little while dividends are usually maintained where possible when profits fall. The dividend therefore gives an important clue as to its sustainable level in the opinion of the board of directors.

Some companies are quite explicit about their dividend policy. For example, the following statement appeared in the 1997 annual report of Rural Press Limited:

"The company's dividend policy is to pay approximately 50% of its after-tax profits to its ordinary and preferred shareholders. This proportion may vary from year to year to ensure that if at all possible, the previous level of dividend is maintained."

This suggests that, instead of thinking about a payout ratio which varies every year, we should try to estimate 'sustainable' profitability and the proportion of 'sustainable' profits which companies will distribute in dividends.

Accordingly, most of the variations in profitability are translated into fluctuations in retained profits rather than fluctuating dividends. As a result, the dividend stream per share tends to be a steadily increasing straight line when plotted on a logarithmic scale. The slope of the line indicates the retained proportion of 'sustainable' profitability.

MEASURING MARKET FLUCTUATIONS IN RELATION TO NET ASSET OR 'BOOK' VALUE

Most of the investigations of market fluctuations have considered market prices on their own unrelated to fundamental accounting data. Where market prices have been used relative to accounting data, significant benefits can be attained. For example, the co-editor of *Risks and Rewards*, the newsletter of the Investment Section of the US Society of Actuaries, provided 'A Toolkit for Estimating Stock Returns' in the July 1996 edition based on dividend yields. In this case fluctuations in dividend yields account for most of the short-term fluctuations in market prices.

In the Autumn 1995 issue of *In the Vanguard*, the newsletter of the Vanguard Group in the USA, the chairman used projections of earnings and price/earnings ratios to provide estimates of 'total return' over the period 1994-2004 on pessimistic, optimistic and 'historical' assumptions, thus enabling investors to compare their expectations in relation to those implicit in market valuations at the end of 1994.

These two examples estimate investment returns by projecting earnings or dividend streams and then applying dividend yields or price/earnings ratios instead of projecting market prices on their own.

A third alternative is use 'price/net-assets' ratios as the main variable. The preference for this approach is based on two principles. The first is accuracy. Earnings forecasts are not renowned for their accuracy, in the case of individual stocks or for a market as a whole. Dividends are more stable but net asset values are more so.

If a company earns 15% on shareholders' funds instead of 10% the error is 50% if one is relying on earnings estimates. Also in this case the dividend may be increased significantly. However, if the typical payout ratio of 60% is maintained, the net asset value would rise to 106% of its previous value instead of 104% and the percentage error in the projected net asset value is only 2%.

The second reason for preferring price/net-assets ratios over price/earnings ratios and dividend yields is the nature of the financial flows between investors and corporations — particularly in raising capital and takeovers.

When a company issues additional shares, the price at which they are issued will be close to ruling prices and the cash raised forms part of shareholders' equity. Consequently this exercise tends to pull market prices and net asset value together.

When companies trade at a discount to net asset value, and the balance sheet values are realistic, they become a target for takeover unless the incumbent management can lift the company's performance and, in so doing, raise its share price.

When companies trade at significant premiums to net asset value, and there are no major hidden or grossly undervalued assets, this is usually caused by high profitability producing above average growth expectations and, in consequence, relatively high price/earnings ratios. In time, high profitability tends to attract competition from entrepreneurs or existing companies in the same business. With some delay, this competition would therefore tend to reduce profitability and, in the process, the excessive premium over net assets value.

Stated net asset value, or shareholders' funds per share, tends to be conservative and may often omit the value of 'intellectual capital' and 'brand loyalty' even though net assets may include intangible assets such as goodwill. Some premium above net asset value should therefore be regarded as normal. Nevertheless, there are observable activities occurring regularly which tend to draw market prices to a modest premium over net asset value. On the other hand there is no rational reason, other than experience, why price/earnings ratios should be 7, 10, 15, 18, 20 or any other particular figure.

The table below shows the ratio of share price to net tangible assets for 10 stocks at five yearly intervals from 1947 to 1977.

Ratio of Market Price to Reported Net Tangible Assets as of 31 December

	1947	1952	1957	1962	1967	1972	1977	Av
ACI	2.28	1.49	1.26	1.76	1.36	1.04	0.52	1.28
Bank of NSW	1.07	1.01	1.05	1.29	1.64	1.95	0.81	1.21
BHP	1.75	1.25	1.28	1.18	3.40	1.52	0.71	1.43
CSR	1.52	1.02	1.02	0.88	1.41	1.76	0.87	1.17
Herald	2.95	1.70	2.69	3.44	3.90	3.73	1.89	2.78
ICI Aust	1.28	1.52	1.90	1.25	1.12	1.04	0.75	1.22
Myer	1.38	0.65	1.54	3.18	3.05	2.35	1.16	1.67
National Bank	1.13	0.84	1.03	1.14	1.50	1.56	0.98	1.14
Repco	2.14	1.01	1.85	1.80	1.91	1.95	0.90	1.58
Woolworths	3.92	2.36	2.51	1.66	1.42	1.53	1.53	2.00
Average	**1.78**	**1.20**	**1.52**	**1.60**	**1.89**	**1.72**	**0.95**	**1.49**

This data was used in an article published in the March 1979 edition of JASSA — the Journal of the Securities Institute of Australia — to support an argument that market indices tended to fluctuate about 1.5 times a market aggregate price-to-net-tangible-assets ratio. The average, 'av', is a geometric average.

Some companies showed price/net-asset ratios which are consistently higher than average — notably *Herald and Weekly Times*. In this case the company employed a deliberate policy of conservatism. In 1973 Alan Geddes was to write:

"Herald and Weekly Times has a quaint practice of writing down its investments in other newspapers to par."

This illustrates the point of being careful with individual price/net-asset figures, even though the majority fall within a range of 1.5 plus or minus 25% — or 1.2 to 1.9. This provides an empirical estimate of the 'normal' range based on accounting practices in use in this period.

To return to the March 1979 JASSA article, there appears to be little relationship — serial correlation — between aggregate price/net-asset ratios at five-yearly intervals. Consequently, when the aggregate price/net-assets ratio is relatively low, the expected capital appreciation over the following five years or so is above average and also, when price/net-assets ratios are low, dividend yields tend to be above average.

Conversely, when price/net-assets ratios are relatively high, dividend yields tend to be lower than historic norms. The US stock market throughout 1997 was a noticeable example of this phenomenon.

Let us now be a little provocative and use the simple formulae which are derived above, adjusted for estimated changes in the price to book ratio, to estimate the total return of the Standard & Poors 500 index over the 10 years to December 2006.

At the start of the period, the dividend yield was 2%. The price to book ratio was 5 compared to a 70-year average of 1.7. Profitability was 23% compared to a 70-year average of 12.5%.[19] It seems most unlikely that this level of profitability will last forever and all experience to date suggests that we should assume it reverts to the historic norm within (say) five years. On this basis, the compound average profitability over the 10 years would be 15% per annum. Also the payout ratio, currently 40%, is a little low by historic norms and would probably rise if profitability fell suggesting a figure of 50% as an average for the 10-year period. This gives an estimated compound average growth rate of 7.5% which added to the dividend yield of 2% gives a 'basic' estimate of 9.5% for total return.

However, if the price to book ratio were to fall to 1.7 this would lead to an adjustment of minus 10%[20] per annum and the total return over the 10 year period would be **minus** 0.5% per annum. While this may be the best 'point estimate' the interested reader may like to redo the calculations on the assumption that the price to book ratio falls to 3.0 which, even at this reduced level, is still high by historical standards.

It is clear that US investors purchasing the 'average portfolio' during 1997, as represented by the S&P 500 index, were not doing their calculations this way! Perhaps this should be left to history to offer judgement in 10 years' time, with the forecasting brilliance enjoyed by hindsight.

THE RELATIONSHIP BETWEEN RISK AND RETURN

Before discussing the relationship between risk and return, some consideration needs to be given to the meaning of the word 'risk'. There does not seem to be much dispute with the idea that the purchase of shares with a time horizon of less than 12 months is speculative.

In the case of short-term speculation, fluctuations will determine the success or failure of the 'investment' and there is some common sense in the idea that more volatile stocks will offer higher speculative gains and higher risks; conversely, with less volatile stocks. Similar arguments would apply to different asset classes such as fixed-interest securities and property trusts.

In so far as time scale is concerned, there is no clear distinction between speculation and investment and few investors have the luxury of inheriting a portfolio at birth and retaining it until death. Accordingly, a practical time frame for considering share investments seems to be something in excess of five years.

It should be apparent from the previous analysis of returns in relation to net asset or book values that, the higher the price/net-assets ratio at the time of purchase, the greater the chance of relatively lower price/net-assets ratios in future. Accordingly, the higher the price/net-assets ratio, the greater the likelihood of adverse price fluctuations. And from the previous discussion on estimating returns, it would follow that the higher the price/net-assets ratio, the lower the expected return and conversely.

The price/net-assets ratio does need to be handled with care in individual cases, but by considering both future returns and price fluctuations relative to net assets or book value, we arrive at the startling conclusion that, in relation to investment in ordinary shares, **the higher the risk the lower the expected return** and conversely.

So does this inverse relationship between risk and return explain the poor performance of the Australian Stock Exchange All Resources index relative to its All Industrials counterpart?

The short answer to this question is probably 'no'. The Resources index is more volatile than the Industrials index, but this does not make it more risky. Its poor performance relative to the Industrials index is likely to be due to relative overvaluation in December 1979 when the index commenced (remember the 'resources boom'?) and/or lower profitability in the resources sector.

When experienced practitioners talk about resource stocks being more risky than industrials, they are principally talking about greater stock price volatility and more volatile earnings. It is possible that people who invest in resource stocks do not build a sufficient margin of safety into their forward estimates of profits, in which case resource stocks would be consistently overpriced, but this possibility would need a great deal of thought before we could conclude, from the relatively poor performance over 1979-1996, that resource stocks should be avoided as a matter of policy.

The principal conclusion from this discussion is that, in aggregate market terms, a relatively high price/net-assets ratio indicates higher risk and lower returns than historical norms. Extending this general principle to individual stocks or groups of stocks requires a certain amount of care.

This discussion would not be complete without comment on the academically fashionable explanation for the poor performance of resource stocks over the last 25 years or so. A number of theorists have suggested that resource stocks should be looked at in an international context and when this is done their *beta* values are lower than the *beta* values of industrial stocks. According to this explanation, Australian resource stocks are less risky than industrials in an international context and consequently international investors are prepared to pay higher prices than Australian investors leading to lower returns for Australian investors.

If this is correct then resource stocks will be permanently overpriced. From the basic buy and hold formula, we know that if the prices of resource stocks are persistently double what they should be, their dividend yield will be (say) 2.5% instead of 5%. And as a result the total return will be 2.5% per annum lower than it should be. But the difference has been considerably more than this. Accordingly, the 'international beta value' argument is, at best, only part of the explanation.

SHARES VERSUS PROPERTY AND BONDS; THE RISK–PREMIUM PUZZLE

The idea that risk and return are inversely related when investing in ordinary shares cannot necessarily be extended to a comparison of shares with bonds.

Also invalid is the widely held view that volatility and return are related, implying the existence of a 'risk' premium for ordinary shares which is then used to justify a preference for shares over bonds.

According to Robert Haugen:[21]

"... financial economists have been struggling to explain the magnitude of the premium to equities relative to Treasury bills in the context of models based on rational economic behaviour."

If investors do not behave rationally and there is no relationship between volatility and return, then why have shares produced significantly higher returns than Treasury bills on a long-term basis?

Using the basic formula for return on a long-term buy and hold strategy, we see that shares will outperform Treasury bills, broadly speaking, if corporate profitability exceeds the average interest rate available on bills.

If this were not the case then shares would have to be consistently priced at a fraction of net asset value to produce a comparable return, public corporations would be unable to raise equity capital and the private sector would more or less disappear.

In other words, the relative performance of shares in relation to fixed-interest securities over the long term depends on the difference between corporate profitability and interest rates. If corporate profitability does not exceed interest rates then it will be impossible for shares to outperform Treasury bills on a long-term basis. The long-term performance of shares relative to bonds is therefore a question involving broad economic issues; it has little to do with stock market volatility and the fluctuating sanity of portfolio investors.

It has become traditional in academic and 'asset consulting' circles to say that property assets are less volatile than shares and more volatile than bonds, **therefore** the long-term return from property should lie between shares and bonds. In certain circumstances, this conclusion is correct, but the reasoning is not.

If, for the moment, we leave aside the effect of inflation on ordinary shares, the nature of the return from shares and property is quite different. The total return from ordinary shares depends, in the long run, on profitability. In the case of property, the long-term return depends on rent and inflation. If there is no inflation, there will be minimal long-term underlying capital appreciation other than fluctuations arising from supply and demand and in the meantime buildings will deteriorate even if the land on which they are built appreciates.

In general, property investors have, in the past, shown themselves to be content with income yields less than the profitability that the corporate sector has been able to achieve. In periods of low inflation, shares should therefore do better than property in the long term. At times of double-digit inflation however, corporations have found it difficult to achieve a return on capital that has exceeded inflation by more than a narrow margin whereas property assets have offered immediate income yields around 10%.

In the long run, the relative performance of shares and property therefore depends on future inflation. Without the benefit of hindsight, long-term inflation has proved to be difficult to forecast with any reliability. As with the relative performance of shares and bonds, the relative returns from property compared to shares is also a broad economic question which has little to do with stock market volatility and rationality among portfolio investors.

SHARES AND INFLATION

This discussion on estimating relative returns from shares, bonds and property would not be complete without an analysis of the effect of inflation on ordinary shares. In the formula for the basic buy and hold strategy, there was no mention of inflation.

All that can be done is to repeat the arguments contained in Chapter 3 and present some additional information. The arguments presented here claim that, without diluting proprietors' interests by issuing additional shares, long-term growth in equity capital, earnings and therefore dividends can only arise from retained profits.

Under historical cost-accounting procedures, there will be an illusory inflationary component of stocks which is counted as profit and included in reported earnings. Similarly, depreciation provisions will be inadequate to provide for the replacement cost of plant and equipment. Accordingly stocks and plant and equipment may be 'real' items, but they are treated as 'monetary' items when profits are calculated. In consequence it is only the monetary value of shareholders' funds which is maintained before determining profits — not the 'real' value.

There are some exceptions to this argument. For example, some companies in the US use last-in-first-out procedures for calculating cost of sales which reduces the illusory effect of stock inflation. In Australia, revaluations of property assets, which in aggregate represent around 30% of shareholders' funds, are usually treated as abnormal items and excluded from profitability calculations.

If a company's business is growing at a faster rate than its retained profits in relation to shareholders' funds, this can be accommodated for a while but gearing ratios will soon be stretched beyond the point at which loan capital becomes available on reasonable terms unless additional equity capital is raised.

Provided profitability and payout ratios remain reasonably stable at around 10% and 60%, then the rate of increase of shareholders' funds should be roughly 4% plus 30% of the rate of inflation in Australian conditions. Subject to fluctuations, this growth rate should be translated into company profits, dividends and share prices.

The table below shows the compound rate of growth of Australian share prices over 104 years prior to the introduction of the new indices in 1979, split into two periods of approximately 50 years each:

Sydney All Ordinaries Index 1875–1979 and Inflation

	1875-1933 (% p.a.)	1933-1979 (% p.a.)
Inflation	0.5	5.0
Index growth	4.1	5.0

It is sometimes argued that this data is very old, but does the fact that the calculations were performed without calculating machines and computers make them any less reliable? Were the people who did these calculations any less capable than the terminal operators and computer programmers of today?

If the broad accuracy of this data is accepted then it shows a significant difference in inflation of 4.5% per annum but only a minor difference in the long-term growth of share prices over corresponding extended periods.

If there is any truth in the second principal argument in favour of shares as an inflation hedge — that corporate assets are 'real' and share prices should reflect this in the long run — then shareholders' funds should still increase from retained profits of (say) 4% per annum. If inflation was an additional factor then why did Australian share prices only increase by 5% per annum and not 9% per annum over the period 1933-1979?

US data leads to a similiar conclusion. The graph below shows a chart of the Standard and Poors 500 dividends per share over the period 1936 to 1995. This graph shows a few bumps, but it is as close as one gets to a straight line in the investment business and the growth rate is well short of what would be expected if inflation was a favourable factor, as well as retained profits. This graph supports the argument that retained profits of the order of 5% per annum of shareholders' funds is the principal cause of dividend growth and, over a long enough period to iron out fluctuations, share prices as well.

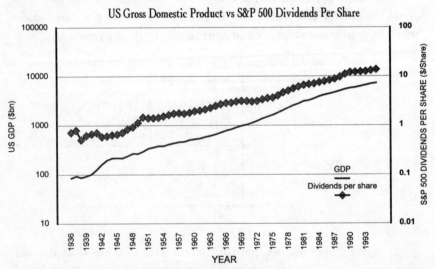

US Gross Domestic Product vs S&P 500 Dividends Per Share

Also shown in the graph above is US Gross Domestic Product which, it will be noted, has increased at a greater rate than the dividend stream — 10% per annum vs 6% per annum. Accordingly, available US data does not support the second principal argument in favour of shares as an inflation hedge — that corporate profits, dividends and therefore share prices should move with Gross Domestic Product.

On the contrary, this discrepancy between dividend growth and Gross Domestic Product supports the more general objection that the idea of dividends moving in parallel ignores the dilutionary effect of capital raising.

The more or less complete elimination of the importance of inflation as a factor affecting the long-term performance of shares reinforces the importance of theorists paying particular attention to profitability which, together with corporate dividend policy, affects the underlying growth of corporate balance sheets as well as the way in which markets value balance sheets and earnings.

Chapter 9

Miscellaneous Issues

CAPITAL GAINS TAX

DEPENDING ON the reader's prejudices, the rationale for the introduction of capital gains tax may have been reasonable — capital gains in excess of that which can be contributed to inflation represents real income to an investor and should therefore be taxed.

Unfortunately, its implementation has been far from fair. To begin with, investors with a mixed portfolio of shares are taxed heavily on the one or two winners, but are not allowed to offset real losses, only monetary ones.

Consider an investor with two securities. Let us suppose they both have the same cost base of $5,000 and the same indexed cost base of $10,000. Security A is sold for $15,000 and security B is sold for $5,000.

According to the theory on which the introduction of capital gains tax was based this investor owns, in total, two securities worth $20,000 with a combined indexed cost base of $20,000. The investor has therefore made nothing more than inflation on his portfolio as a whole. Yet the sale of A for $25,000 leads to a taxable gain of $5,000 but the sale of B for $15,000 leads to no offsetting tax loss. The investor is therefore subject to a taxable gain of $5,000 even though, in total, there was no net realised gain in excess of inflation.

A second unfair aspect of the legislation is the way in which, in a sequence of transactions, taxable gains and losses can leave an investor out-of-pocket even if there is no net realisable gain. This is because investors who make profits in one tax year are taxed, but an equal loss the following year can only be offset against future profits not past ones.

Let us suppose that an investor incurs a capital loss of $10,000 on 30 June and a capital profit of $10,000 on 1 July. In this case the $10,000 loss can be carried forward to the next tax year commencing on 1 July and there would be no net taxable gain. If, on the other hand, the profit is incurred on 30 June and the loss one day later on 1 July, the profit would be taxed and as the loss is incurred the following tax year it will need to be carried forward until such time as the investor has taxable gains to absorb the loss.

Finally, there is the question as to whether the tax achieves anything in relation to long-term investors in shares other than double taxation of company profits anyway. As discussed earlier, share prices rise in the long term because of retained profits — not inflation — and these profits have already borne corporate tax. Why should they be taxed again?

Similarly, property values generally fall in real terms as buildings age. So, once again the revenue from long-term capital gains is likely to be minimal.

The proponents of capital gains taxes might argue that because the likely revenue is minimal, no-one should have much to complain about. So what is the problem? Those who have sold any investments over the last few years will know of the extensive and detailed records which are required to be kept.

The various 'initiatives' in the taxation, superannuation and corporate legislation areas in the late 1980s and early 1990s led to a substantial increase in the demand for lawyers and accountants — so much so that a large number of potentially outstanding young people may have been diverted to these professions for financial reasons. A political, taxation and financial system which creates such a reward structure needs to have its priorities questioned.

SUPERANNUATION

Australians are staying in the education system longer, living longer and having fewer children. These demographic changes are expected to substantially increase the ratio of those members of the population who are dependent for their livelihood on those who provide it over the next 50 years. Left unchecked this will place a great deal of additional financial pressure on the working population.

To deal with this problem, superannuation funds, in the apparent opinion of the government, are essential. If the cause of the problem is demographic, one wonders why a dramatic and compulsory increase in the amount of money in superannuation funds will solve the problem.

The real solution is to change working patterns so that the ratio of people in the 'dependant' population does not reach a level at which the members of the 'productive' population are not prepared to support the demands of the 'dependant' population. To some extent the changes necessary to support this demographic change have begun to emerge — less rigid retirement ages, flexible working hours and permanent part-time jobs.

The noted author of US management texts, Peter F. Drucker, was reported to have suggested that fiddling with taxes and social security is making the problem worse in some countries by causing a declining birth rate. According to Drucker the retirement age in developed countries will need to rise to 75 to resolve this issue:[1]

"The reproductive rate is down to almost 1 in southern Europe and about 1.5 in Japan. ...

"There won't be enough people to work. There'll only be older people. There won't be enough producers.

"The main reason for the decline in births is the enormous burden on people of working age supporting older people in retirement who are hale and hearty. You cannot cut [Social Security payments] of older people because that's the law.

"So they [the Europeans] cut where they have control, which is having babies. ...

"The retirement age in all developed countries will have to go up to 75. Most people who reach 65 are still capable of functioning. All present talk of financing Social Security is beside the point. The point is not money. The point is production."

While the tax advantages of superannuation were substantially reduced in the early 1990s, it seems unlikely that the taxation regime applying to superannuation funds will ever be more onerous than that endured by private individuals. For this reason, serious investors should consider establishing their own fund so as to achieve more direct control over their superannuation. This will cost a little, particularly in the early stages, but this cost will be partly offset by avoiding the various 'up-fronts' and 'on-goings' charged by public funds. This comment also applies to employees of large companies with in-house superannuation funds when they change jobs.

The general push towards superannuation in Australia and the experience of beneficiaries of the Maxwell pension funds in the UK, caused a mild panic in government circles about the safety of money held in superannuation funds. It was not difficult to forecast that the result would be regulation which significantly increased the expenses of running superannuation funds. History also suggests that the regulation will not work when it is most needed.

One other aspect of superannuation which is worth mentioning is its changing nature. Many years ago a pension for life used to be a reward for loyal and faithful service to the one employer over decades. This perception is changing. These days the cost of superannuation is becoming increasingly regarded as a deferred part of an employee's remuneration. Consequently, there has been a drift from funds with benefits defined in terms of salary and years of service to funds where the employer agrees to pay a fixed percentage of salary.

As this trend develops employees will increasingly begin to regard their superannuation as 'their money' and will insist on it being invested outside their employers' control. Member choice will be a powerful force in the future.

SURVIVING ON AN INVESTMENT PORTFOLIO

In recent years there have been times when it has been possible to buy short-term fixed-interest securities at yields of around 20% per annum. It was also possible to earn 15% per annum and more with bank security. In such times, the rate of inflation was well above zero and consequently people who treated the whole interest payment as 'income' were in effect eroding the real value of their capital.

This illustrates the important point that in inflationary conditions the distinction between income and capital is by no means black and white. In these circumstances, treating interest as income is a delusion — and in this respect taxation laws are quite unfair.

From the investor's point of view, income should be the increase in value of a portfolio over a period allowing for inflation, taxation, dividends etc. received, and drawings. This is not easy to measure, particularly as it involves changes in value as distinct from price.

An investor who spends income thus defined will be maintaining the real value (and therefore the income-generating capacity) of the underlying portfolio.

The next question is what real after-tax income can an investor reasonably expect in the long run from a portfolio. Some years ago, this question was considered by the High Court[2] in connection with calculating lump sum compensation for loss of earnings as a result of injury. The answer was 3% per annum. On this basis, and using round figures to keep the arithmetic simple, a young retiree who aspires to a lifestyle which requires $35,000 per annum to support (and with no other income) needs an investment portfolio of $1 million.

One other factor which needs to be taken into account is that apart from medical bills, most living expenses tend to decrease with age in retirement. A retiree dependent on an investment portfolio can therefore afford to spend a little more than 3% per annum of the value of the underlying portfolio — assuming the figure of 3% is correct in the first place.

At the risk of proposing a novel formula which has not worn the test of time, the appropriate percentage for men is age divided by 12. Women should deduct five years from their age (because they live longer than men) and divide the result by 12. Thus a man retiring at 60 proposing to survive on an investment portfolio could regard 5% of the value of his portfolio as annual 'income' or spending money.

Finally, it might be appropriate to provide some practical advice on implementing these ideas. The first step is to completely segregate bank or other accounts used for investment purposes from those used for living expenses. An investment account is used to collect dividends, etc., pay income tax and for share purchases. In addition, there should be a standing order to transfer a regular amount each month from the investment account to an account kept for living expenses. The amount of this regular transfer should be established and reviewed from time to time in the light of the discussion above.

This segregation has a number of advantages. Income and dividend payments tend to be seasonal and irregular whereas most living expenses are regular and stable. Making a regular transfer therefore makes household budgeting easier. Investment accounts tend to have low levels of activity and a different sort of account may be advantageous — for example cheque access may not be necessary. Also, taxable receipts will not be passing through an account with high levels of activity which makes it easier to collect information required for preparation of tax returns.

The figures used here are based on achieving reasonable investment results. Most people would expect to be able to do somewhat better. Without wishing to dent readers' enthusiasm, it should be recognised that achieving above-average investment results eludes a great many intelligent and highly-paid professional investors. The average retiree may therefore be optimistic in assuming better than average investment results. If this proves to be conservative then the periodic review of the amount to be regularly transferred enables good results to be rewarded after they have been achieved rather than anticipated. There is no shortage of people who thought they could achieve above average investment results before they discovered how difficult this was.

CONCENTRATION AND INSTABILITY

An essential part of any investment program is diversification. This is a policy which has worked well for investors for centuries and investors who put all or most of their money in apparently outstanding opportunities like Pyramid Building Society have paid a heavy price.

Although the legislation governing superannuation funds is intended to be tight, the possibility of disaster is still present.[3] There is always going to be the risk of gross misappropriation of money from any fund. If a person's whole superannuation is tied up in the fund concerned the experience could be disastrous.

If, on the other hand, superannuation entitlements are held in a number of different funds, then misappropriation of one fund would hurt without being totally disastrous.

Consequently, all superannuants over the age of (say) 50, from which recovery from total loss would be difficult, may feel more comfortable with their superannuation held in more than one fund with different and separate trustees.

This problem of concentration of risk goes a great deal further than the principle of diversification for individual investors. It has far-reaching effects on the financial system and political institutions. The damage that has been done by centralised decision-making in the last few years is considerable — 'performance'-chasing leading up to the crash of 1987, the effect of research houses' recommendations on unlisted property trusts, and the wild debt spree of the late 1980s in which government-controlled institutions were actively involved.

In his book about the Japanese Ministry of Finance[4], Peter Hartcher demonstrates how an elite bureaucracy rose to become so powerful that it was almost unaccountable to its minister. Yet, this organisation appeared to have been responsible for monumental blunders which, according to Hartcher, threatened the world financial system.

In 1997, the Australian government apparently accepted most of the recommendations of an inquiry into the Australian financial system (named the 'Wallis report' after its chairman) including a proposal to concentrate the prudential supervision of most financial institutions under one roof. What happens if this mega-regulator catches 'groupthink' and, as a result, the Australian financial system becomes as accident prone as its Japanese counterpart?

History has demonstrated that there are only two reliable safeguards for investors: diversification and vigilance. People should not have all their money in one basket and they should be wary of all advice they receive. Any legislative or company requirement which requires people to have all their money in one fund is dangerous. Equally dangerous is the existence of government licences or registrations which (unintentionally) encourage people to drop their guard.

To counter this concentration of control, the illusion of regulatory safety, and the dangers of groupthink, individual citizens may need to become more knowledgeable on investment matters, take an increased interest in the conduct of their affairs and become self-sufficient in their approach.

Self-sufficiency includes an ability to critically evaluate all ideas and arguments which the investor encounters, including those presented in *BluePrint for Investment*.

Notes and References

Chapter 1 INTRODUCTION – DIFFERENT APPROACHES TO INVESTMENT THEORY AND PRACTICE

1. *Money Management*, 18 June 1992.
2. Dunstan, Barrie, *The Art of Investment*, John Fairfax Group Pty Ltd, 1991 p. vii.
3. Such as *Investments* by W. F. Sharpe, Prentice Hall, 1978.
4. Sharpe, William F. and Alexander, Gordon J., *Investments*, Prentice Hall, 1990 p. 80.
5. Sharpe, William F., *Investments*, Prentice-Hall, 1978 p. 119.
6. Train, John, *The Midas Touch*, Harper & Row, 1987 p. 50.
7. Geddes, Alan, *Investment in a Changing World*, Rydge Publications, 1974 p. 74.
8. Donnelly, Austin, *The Three R's of Investing*, Second Edition, Allen & Unwin, 1987 p. 11.
9. *Superannuation Investments – A Guide for Trustees*, Wrightbooks 1992.
10. Donnelly, Austin, 1987 *op cit* p. 11.
11. Fama, Eugene F. and French, Kenneth R., The Cross-Section of Expected Stock Returns, *The Journal of Finance*, Vol. XLVII No. 2, June 1992 pp. 427-465.
12. *Fortune Magazine*, 1 June 1992.
13. As measured by the standard deviations of continuously compounded monthly rates of return. To obtain annual volatility, multiply by $\sqrt{12}$.
14. Black, Fischer, *The Journal of Finance*, Vol. XLI, No. 3 July 1986.
15. See for example Taylor, Stephen, *Modelling Financial Time Series*, John Wiley 1986.
16. Cottle S., Murray R.F. and Block F.E., *Graham and Dodd's Security Analysis*, 1988 Fifth Edition, McGraw Hill.
17. Buffett, Warren E., "The Superinvestors of Graham-and-Doddsville", *Hermes, Magazine of Columbia Business School*, Fall 1984. Reprinted in *The Intelligent Investor* by Benjamin Graham, Fourth Revised Edition pp. 291-313.

18. Dreman, David N., *The New Contrarian Investment Strategy*, Random House, 1982 pp. 139-152.

19. Fama, Eugene F. and French, Kenneth R., "Dividend Yields and Expected Stock Returns", *Journal of Financial Economics*, 1988 Vol. 22 No. I pp.3-25.

20. *The Australian Financial Review*, 4 February 1997.

21. Buffett, Warren E., *op cit* 1984 p. 300.

22. Keynes, John Maynard, *The General Theory of Employment Interest and Money*, (1936) Reprint 1970, MacMillan p. 154.

23. Platinum Capital Limited, December 1996 half yearly report.

24. Maley, Karen, *The Australian Financial Review*, 6 February 1997.

25. Colebatch, Tim, *The Age*, 1 March 1997.

26. Westpac Investment Management Ltd, promotional brochure, September 1988.

27. Australian Eagle Life Insurance Company. *The Principle of Sound Investing – Risk Related Return*, apparently published in 1987.

28. The Assessment of Investment Pools, *Quarterly Journal of The Institute Of Actuaries of Australia*, December 1988.

29. Barker, M.D., Application of Option Pricing Theory to Superannuation Funds, *Transactions of the Institute of Actuaries of Australia*, 1989 p. 1217.

30. *The Australian Financial Review*, 27 August 1987.

31. Dreman, David N., *Psychology and the Stock Market*, Amacom 1977.

32. Janis, Irving, *Victims of Groupthink*, Houghton Mifflin 1972.

33. *Business Review Weekly*, 9 October 1992.

34. Galbraith, J.K., *The Great Crash 1929*, Penguin 1975 p. 11.

35. Lynch, Peter, *One Up on Wall Street*, Simon & Schuster 1989 p.32.

36. Train, John, *The Money Masters*, Harper and Row 1980.

37. Train, John, *The New Money Masters*, Harper and Row 1989.

38. Train, John, *The Midas Touch*, Harper & Row 1987.

39. Train, *op cit* 1980.

40. *Ibid*, p. 246.

41. Geddes, Alan, 1974 *op cit* p. 14.

Chapter 2 THE LESSONS OF HISTORY

1. Brown, A. and Thompson, J.E., "1,2 or 3 Investment managers? Some thoughts on split funding", *Transactions of The Institute of Actuaries of Australia*, 1988 p. 76.

2. Sykes, Trevor, *Two Centuries of Panic*, Allen & Unwin 1988.
3. Binns, J. D., *Institutional Investment*, The Institute of Actuaries (London) 1965.
4. Geddes, Alan, *Investment in a Changing World*, Rydge Publications, 1974 p. 14.
5. Lowenstein, Rodger, *Buffett*, Random House 1995 p. 161.
6. Sykes, Trevor, *The Money Miners*, Allen & Unwin 1995.
7. *Ibid*, Preface and Introduction to 1995 Edition.
8. Sykes, Trevor, *op cit* 1988.
9. Pizzo, Stephen, Fricker, Mary and Muolo, Paul, *Inside Job*, McGraw-Hill 1989.
10. Mackay, Charles, *Memoirs of Extraordinary Popular Delusions and the Madness of Crowds*, Harmony Books, 1980 Reprint p. 90.
11. *Ibid*, pp. 89-97.
12. Aden-Ayales, Pamela and Aden-Harter, Mary Anne, *Aden Gold Study*, 3rd printing, Adam Smith publishing, Metairie LA 1981.
13. M.W. Comment, "Penny Stocks and Five-thousand-dollar gold", *Metals Week*, 8 October 1979 p. 5.
14. *The Echo*, Geelong, 26 August 1992.
15. *The Weekly Times*, 20 September 1989.
16. *The Weekly Times*, 23 September 1992.
17. *Australian Ostrich Journal*, September 1992.
18. *The Weekly Times*, 5 March 1997 p. B19.
19. Galbraith, J.K., *The Great Crash 1929*, Penguin 1975.
20. *The Sunday Age*, 5 April 1992.
21. Hale, Brian, *The Australian Financial Review*, 20 January 1997.
22. Wyatt, John, The Incredible Death-Defying Stock Market, *Fortune*, 23 December 1996 pp. 68-73.
23. *Ibid*, p.72.
24. This point is discussed at some length by US author Richard Band in *Contrary Investing for the 90s*, Alexandria House 1989.
25. "Top US Investor Warns on Wall St", *The Age*, 17 March 1997 p. B1.
26. Ross, Gavin, quoted in *The Sunday Age*, February 1994.
27. Band, Richard E., *Contrary Investing for the '90s*, Alexandria House, 1989.
28. Nomura Securities Co. Ltd, *The Australian*, 31 January 1989 p. 7.
29. *The Australian Financial Review*, 3 April 1992.
30. Wyatt, *op cit*, 1996 p. 73.

31. Australian Law Reform Commission, Discussion Paper 53, "Collective Investment Schemes", October 1992.

32. House of Representatives Standing Committee on Financial Institutions and Public Administration, Public hearing in relation to the Australian Securities Commission Annual Report 1995-1996, Sydney, 29 January 1997, transcript p. 6.

33. Bosch, Henry, "The Adventures of Tricontinental", *Stock Exchange Journal*, November 1992.

34. 'Pierpont', "It all boils down to a matter of trust", *The Australian Financial Review*, 8 November 1996.

35. Band, Richard E., *op cit.*

Chapter 3 GENERAL FEATURES OF DIFFERENT ASSET CLASSES

1. Investment Property Research Pty Ltd, *Property Trust Monitor*, March 1997.

2. Dreman, David N., *The New Contrarian Investment Strategy*, Random House 1982.

3. In fact, contracts can be cleared more than once per day if there is unusually large volatility.

4. *A Guide to the Clearing and Financial Integrity of the Sydney Futures Exchange*, Sydney Futures Exchange Limited 1995.

5. Galbraith, J. K., *The Great Crash 1929*, Penguin 1975.

6. Oxford Dictionary.

7. In one particular area of NSW, regularly overflown by aircraft inbound to Canberra, the view became so pock-marked by 'tax deductible dams' that it became known as 'Little Venice'.

8. Blundell, G., *The Actuary*, 1995.

9. Graham, Benjamin, *The Intelligent Investor* Fourth Revised Edition p. 21.

Chapter 4 INVESTMENT OBJECTIVES AND STRATEGY; FORMULATION, IMPLEMENTATION AND SUPERVISION

1. *Superannuation Industry (Supervision) Act*, 1993.

2. For a detailed account see Sykes, Trevor, *The Money Miners*, Allen & Unwin, 1995 (reprint) pp. 236-301.

3. Geddes, Alan, *Investment in a Changing World*, Rydges 1974 pp. 51-52.

4. Sykes, Trevor, *Two Centuries of Panic*, Allen & Unwin 1988 pp. 411-433.

5. Loeb, Gerald M., *The Battle for Investment Survival*, Simon & Schuster 1965, p. 27.

6. *Ibid*, pp. 27-31.

7. Keynes, John Maynard, *The General Theory of Employment Interest and Money*, Paperback (reprint) 1970, pp. 154-155.

8. *Ibid*, p. 157.

9. *Ibid*, p. 158.

10. *Superannuation Industry (Supervision) Act* 1993.

11. Fisher, H. F. and Young, J. *The Actuarial Practice of Life Assurance*, Cambridge University Press 1965 pp. 167-172.

12. Barker, M. D., "Should funds take bigger risks?", *JASSA – Journal of the Securities Institute of Australia*, June 1992.

13. Reprinted in Graham, Benjamin, *The Intelligent Investor*, *op cit* p. I.

14. Association of Superannuation Funds of Australia, *Superannuation Investments – A Guide For Trustees*, Wrightbooks 1992.

15. Buffett, Warren E., *Berkshire Hathaway Inc. Chairman's Letter*, 27 February 1997.

16. *Property Trust Monitor*, published monthly by Property Investment Research Pty Ltd, is a valuable source of information for investors in this sector.

Chapter 5 INVESTORS' INTERESTS, CORPORATE GOVERNANCE AND THE INVESTMENT INDUSTRY

1. Geddes, Alan, *Investment in a Changing World*, Rydges 1974 p. 41.

2. Townsend, Robert, *Up the Organisation*, Coronet Books, 1971.

3. Rivett, Patrick, *Principles of Model Building*, John Wiley 1971, pp. 117-120.

4. Fama, Eugene F. and French, Kenneth R. "The Cross-Section of Expected Stock Returns", *The Journal of Finance*, Vol. XLVII No. 2, June 1992 pp. 427-465.

5. Renton, N. E., *Company Directors: Masters or Servants?*, Wrightbooks 1994.

6. *Ibid*, p. 152.

7. *Ibid*, p. 154.

8. *The Australian Financial Review*, 20 March 1996 p. 25.

9. Australian Securities Commission, *Don't Kiss Your Money Goodbye, How to Choose a Financial Adviser*, 1992.

10. Australian Securities Commission, *Review of the Licensing Regime for Securities Advisers*, Issues Paper, February 1995.

11. House of Representatives Standing Committee on Financial Institutions and Public Administration, Public hearing in relation to the Australian Securities Commission Annual Report 1995-1996, Sydney 29 January 1997, transcript p.7.

12. *Ibid*, p. 7.

13. Donnelly, Austin, *The Three R's of Investing*, Second Edition Allen & Unwin, 1987 Preface.

14. *Australian Investors Association Ltd*, 1996 Annual Report.

15. Ball, Ray; Brown, Phillip and Finn, Frank J., *Published investment recommendations and share prices: are there any free lunches in security analysis?* JASSA, June 1978.

16. *Corporations Law* 1989, Section 585.

17. Borradale, Anna, "Just a case of boutique bashing", *Money Management*, 5 November 1992 p. 11.

18. Regular checkups are the best medicine, *Personal Investment*, November 1992 p. 24.

19. Borradale, Anna, *op cit* 1992.

Chapter 6 PACKAGED FINANCIAL PRODUCTS AND INDIRECT INVESTMENT

1. "Regular check-ups are the best medicine", *Personal Investment*, November 1992 p. 24.

2. Maxilink Limited, *Report to Shareholders*, June 1992 and June 1996; index weightings were extracted from *Companies on the Australian Stock Exchange Indices*, Australian Stock Exchange Limited, June 1996.

3. *Collective Investment Schemes*, Australian Law Reform Commission, Discussion Paper 53, October 1992.

4. "You Can Trust Me, I'm a Fund Manager," *Australian Financial Review*, 5 September 1997 p. 84.

Chapter 7 INVESTING IN LISTED SECURITIES AND UNUSUAL POOLS

1. Stutchbury, O. P., *The Management of Unit Trusts*, Thomas Skinner 1964.
2. Mercantile Mutual Global Property Fund, Prospectus dated 28 September 1992.
3. Roth, Martin, *Analysing Company Accounts*, Wrightbooks, 1995.

Chapter 8 THEORETICAL PRINCIPLES AND CONSIDERATIONS

1. Rivett, Patrick, *Principles of Model Building*, John Wiley, 1972 p. I.
2. Haugen, Robert A. 1995, *The New Finance – The Case Against Efficient Markets*, Prentice-Hall, 1995.
3. *Ibid*, p. 136.
4. *Ibid*, p. 137.
5. Geddes, Alan, *Investment in a Changing World*, Rydges, 1974 p. 75.
6. Clarkson R. S., "Financial Economics – an Investment Actuary's Viewpoint", *British Actuarial Journal*, 1996 Vol. 2, Part IV.
7. *British Actuarial Journal*, 1996 Vol. 2, Part IV. p. 965.
8. Rivett, 1972, *op cit* Preface.
9. Following the paper by Fama and French. Refer Chapter 1 for discussion.
10. Peters, Edgar E., *Chaos and Order in the Capital Markets*, John Wiley, pp. 81-103 1991.
11. "Stochastic Investment Models", *Transactions of The Institute of Actuaries of Australia*, 1992 pp. 213-214.
12. The literature on this point is extensive. An early pioneering study covering British companies in the 1950s was *Higgledy Piggledy Growth Again* by I.M.D. Little and A. C. Rayner, Basil Blackwell, 1966.
13. *Journal of the Institute of Actuaries*, Vol. 101.
14. For a summary of price/earnings studies see *The New Contrarian Investment Strategy* by David Dreman, Random House, 1982 pp. 139-152.
15. Wilkie, A. D., "Can dividend yields predict share price changes?" Transactions of the 3rd International AFIR Colloquium, 1993 Rome 1 pp. 335-347.

16. Fama, Eugene F. and French, Kenneth R., "The Cross-Section of Expected Stock Returns," *The Journal of Finance*, Vol. XLVII No. 2, June 1992 pp. 427-465.

17. Huntley, Ian writing in *Australian Shareholder* (Eleventh Edition p. 1), wrote:

    "*[according to] (Jim) Slater and Peter Lynch] fair value is where the price earnings multiple equals the average percentage growth rate...*"

18. Hemsted, J. R., "The expected yield on ordinary shares". *Journal of the Institute of Actuaries Students Society*. Vol. 16, Part 6 1962. "Cycles and Trends in the Australian Stockmarket". *JASSA Journal of the Securities Institute of Australia*, March 1979.

19. Platinum Capital Limited, *Quarterly Report*, December 1996.

20. *en* { 1.7 / 5.0 } = minus 0.1

21. Haugen, *op cit.*

Chapter 9 MISCELLANEOUS ISSUES

1. *Forbes*, 10 March 1997 p. 126.

2. Todorovich v Waller, *Commonwealth Law Reports*, Vol. 150, 1981.

3. *Australian Financial Review*, September 19, 1997 p. 80.

4. Hartcher, Peter, *The Ministry*, Harper Collins 1997.

Index

Index